Gettysburg's Bloody Wheatfield

By
Jay Jorgensen

WHITE MANE BOOKS
SHIPPENSBURG, PENNSYLVANIA

Cover Illustration: *The Wheatfield* by Paul R. Martin III, ©2001 Courtesy of Silent Sentinel Studio, P.O. Box 551, Yorktown Heights, NY 10598, Phone: 914-245-8903, www.paulmartinart.com, available as a S/N Fine Art Print.

The acid-free paper used in this book meets the guidelines for permanence and durability of the Committee on Production Guidelines for Book Longevity of the Council on Library Resources.

For a complete list of available publications
please write
White Mane Books
Division of White Mane Publishing Company, Inc.
P.O. Box 708
Shippensburg, PA 17257-0708 USA

Library of Congress Cataloging-in-Publication Data

Jorgensen, Jay, 1956-
      Gettysburg's bloody wheatfield / by Jay Jorgensen.
            p. cm.
      Includes bibliographical references and index.
      ISBN-13: 978-1-57249-253-0 ISBN-10: 1-57249-253-8 (alk. paper) --
      ISBN-13: 978-1-57249-360-5 ISBN-10: 1-57249-360-7 (pbk.)
      1. Gettysburg (Pa.), Battle of, 1863. I. Title.

E475.53 .J68 2001
973.7'349--dc21

                                                          2001046927

PRINTED IN THE UNITED STATES OF AMERICA

This book is dedicated to my parents,
Norman and Miriam Jorgensen,
for instilling in me a lifelong love of history,
and to my wife, Maureen,
for her love and all that she does for our family.

Contents

Illustrations

Maps

Preface

When I set out to write this book, one question kept coming up. Why the Wheatfield? The Wheatfield was a pivotal part of the Battle of Gettysburg, yet it has been almost neglected by researchers and historians. The action was relatively short-lived, yet the toll it took was tremendous. While Gettysburg is the most studied and chronicled battle of the Civil War, little is written about this important action that occurred on the second day of the fight.

There is no question that the action in the Wheatfield was confusing. The tide turned several times, huge mistakes were made by commanders, and the carnage left behind was staggering. Even the first person reports by those who fought in this bloody battle are contradictory.

My interest was to try to make sense of this confusing and poorly understood action. I was intrigued by the personalities involved in this battle, but my research revealed that it was the common soldiers who made the difference. Their bravery and courage in the face of terrifying circumstances is a tribute to their commitment.

No one can be certain of what happened in the Wheatfield on July 2, 1863. I believe that this account is as accurate as is possible from a distance of nearly a century and half. I hope to impart to readers a clearer sense of what happened that day, and an appreciation of the tremendous sacrifice made on George Rose's farmstead in a small crossroads town in Pennsylvania.

* * * * *

One of the true pleasures that I have experienced in writing this book is the wonderful cooperation and help of so many people. To obtain a good understanding of the action one has to walk the field itself. I am most appreciative of the wonderful insights imparted during many of my visits by a trio of outstanding Gettysburg Battlefield tour guides: Gary Kross, Tom Prisk, and Trish Murphy. Gary fueled my initial interest in this topic, and he and Tom have always been willing to discuss any and all aspects of the fight with me. I am further indebted to Tom for sharing my passion for this battle and encouraging me to continue on with writing this book. D. Scott Hartwig and Eric Campbell have assisted my research by informing me of the wonderful material available at the Gettysburg National Park Library, as well as taking time out of their busy schedules to talk to me about the Wheatfield.

Steve Zerbe, an extraordinary Civil War researcher, was helpful in tracking down hard-to-find accounts of the Wheatfield action. I was fortunate to have made the acquaintance and friendship of David Evans and Charlotte Ray in Georgia. Both provided me with valuable material on several of the Georgia regiments that fought in the battle, as well as helping me locate additional source materials.

Several people were kind enough to read early drafts of this book, and they all made excellent suggestions for improvements. Edward Hagerty, professor at American Military University, read a portion of this work that was submitted while I was working on my master's degree in military history, Civil War studies, from that university, and his help and guidance were greatly appreciated. Al Gambone provided me with the first overall critique, and pointed out areas of controversy and concern that were most welcome. Mike Snyder read the manuscript very carefully and provided me with detailed suggestions and corrections that have been incorporated into this book.

Civil War artist Paul R. Martin, III, offered to do a special print for the dust jacket. Paul's talents are limitless, and I am most thankful that he volunteered his time and talents to help with the book. Roger Grutzmacher and Joann Montero, outstanding architects in New Jersey, were instrumental in developing the maps for this work. The positives of the maps are attributable to them, the negatives are all mine. A word on the maps. I have included time frames for the action depicted in each map. Establishing times for the Wheatfield fighting is difficult at best, since virtually none of the first-hand accounts reference any specific times. So, the times set forth are my best estimate as to when those events took place, and should be viewed as such. What I really wanted to impart to readers with the maps is the general location of the units that fought in the Wheatfield at different stages of the fighting.

One of the great benefits I received in writing this was the outpouring of genuine interest, support, assistance, and encouragement from so many friends. The following individuals have been especially helpful: Greg Acken, Neal Auricchio, Pat Barnes, Pete Barnes, Rich Bellamy, Bill Bork, Matt Borowick, Carole Capp-Saccocci, Mike Cavanaugh, Stan Domosh, Jim Donovan, Bruce Form, Bob Gaydosh, Karen Kulaga, Paul Lader, John Michael Priest, Jeff Stocker, and Bill Welsch. I am fortunate to have developed long-distance friendships with people across the country who have provided me with research information. In particular, I would like to thank John Griffin, Neal Griffin, Dave Larson, and Ken Woodington from that group. Another person to whom I am indebted in helping with this book is Sue Makwinski, who had the difficult task of reading my handwriting and typing the text.

I am grateful to Elwood Christ and Tim Smith from the Adams County Historical Society for helping to arrange for the use of the Tipton photographs that are contained in this book. I would also like to thank the staffs of the Civil War Library & Museum in Philadelphia, Pennsylvania, and the Civil War Library & Research Center in Woodbridge, New Jersey, for their assistance. Early on in my research I contacted many institutions across the country looking for applicable material.

The following organizations were helpful in their prompt responses: U.S. Army Military Institute, National Archives & Records Administration, Historical Society of Pennsylvania, University of North Carolina, Duke University, Emory University, Indiana State Library, New York Historical Society, University of Texas at Austin, Alabama Department of Archives & History, University of Georgia Library, Henry E. Huntington Library, Louisiana State University, Maryland Historical Society Library, Ohio Historical Society Library, Georgia Department of Archives & History, New Jersey State Archives, Stephen F. Austin State University, and Washington & Lee University.

I wish to thank the folks at White Mane Publishing Company for their assistance. Especially helpful was Alexis Handerahan, who was a terrific editor to work with. I would also like to give a special thanks and gratitude to Civil War historian extraordinaire, Ed Bearss, for taking the time out of his busy schedule to review my book.

Last, but certainly not least, I want to thank my family for their help, support, and love. No father could ever hope for better children than my sons, John and Bob. They have adopted my interest in Gettysburg as their own, and have spent countless hours traipsing the battlefield with me. Indeed, I can ask for no better companions to walk the Wheatfield with than my boys, who have become experts in the intricacies of the battle. As for my wife, Maureen, she is simply the best person in the world. She served many roles throughout this project, including editor, listener, supporter, and encourager. Never once did she even intimate that I was wasting my time working on an event that occurred so long ago, or that I could be spending my time doing something else. Her literary insights were right on target. But, most of all, her assistance made working on this book a joy, and her love, friendship, and companionship makes my life truly wonderful.

Chapter One

The Cream of the Confederacy

The Battle of Gettysburg was one of the defining moments of the American Civil War. General Robert E. Lee's invasion into Pennsylvania with his Army of Northern Virginia culminated in a desperate fight with Major General George Gordon Meade's Army of the Potomac on the first three days of July 1863. When the two armies separated from each other on the evening of the 87th anniversary of the country's Independence Day, 45,364 men had been either killed, wounded, or were missing in action. Lee's army had suffered 22,557 casualties, and its effectiveness as an offensive fighting force had been decimated. But before the battle ended, the Confederates had fought as well as any troops in military history, and the fate of a nation rested on the staunch defense provided by the Federal soldiers on the outskirts of the small borough of Gettysburg.[1]

Although there was fighting between the two armies on all three days, the heaviest action took place on July 2, 1863. The struggle on that day at various locations on the battlefield has given rise to a list of places that are now fixed in American history: Little Round Top, Devil's Den, the Peach Orchard, Culp's Hill, and, the Wheatfield.

The fight in and around the twenty-six acres of wheat owned by local farmer George Rose has been largely overlooked by Gettysburg historians. One of the reasons for this omission is the confusing, overlapping nature of the action. A total of six Confederate brigades battled thirteen Federal brigades during the three and one-half hours of fighting.[2] Units were sent into the fight in piecemeal fashion, making it difficult for any organized analysis. Another reason for the lack of study on the Wheatfield is that neither side had anyone in overall control of the field. For the Federals, troops from four different army corps were engaged, yet none of the corps commanders (except Major General Daniel E. Sickles, who was severely wounded during the action) was present. Of the Federal divisional commanders, only Brigadier General John C. Caldwell exercised any meaningful, hands-on command in the Wheatfield. For the Confederates, only Major General Lafayette McLaws executed command above the brigade level in the fighting.

This book will analyze the fight for the Wheatfield and clarify the confused action that Gettysburg historian Eric Campbell has rightly referred to as "The Whirlpool."[3] This objective will be accomplished by focusing on Brigadier General George T. Anderson's Brigade in Major General John Bell Hood's Division. Major General McLaws's three brigades that engaged the Federals in the waist-high wheat will also be focused on. These brigades were commanded by brigadier generals Joseph B. Kershaw, Paul J. Semmes, and William T. Wofford. I will examine not only how the battle unfolded, but also those factors which led to success and failure in the bloody fighting.

George T. "Tige" Anderson was born in Covington, Georgia, on February 3, 1824. While matriculating at Emory College in Oxford, Georgia, Anderson felt compelled to leave school and fight for his state and country in the Mexican War. As a lieutenant of a Georgia cavalry regiment, he served under the command of General Stephen W. Kearney. After the war he returned to Georgia, married Elizabeth Ramey, and took up the family occupation of farming. In 1855, he received a commission as captain in Colonel Joseph E. Johnston's 1st U.S.

Cavalry, and served with that regiment in Kansas. Resigning his commission in 1858, he remained in Kansas until Georgia seceded from the Union, whereupon Anderson returned to his native state. He immediately helped raise a company in Walton County, and was elected captain. Upon the organization of the 11th Georgia in July 1861, Anderson was elected its colonel. He immediately took his regiment to Virginia, where he reported to his old 1st U.S. Cavalry commander, General Joseph E. Johnston, at Manassas. Anderson was given command of a brigade, consisting of the 7th, 8th, 9th, and 11th Georgia regiments and the 1st Kentucky. On November 1, 1862, he was promoted to brigadier general, and served in that capacity with the Army of Northern Virginia through the end of the war.

Returning to Georgia after Appomattox, Anderson worked for a railroad. From 1877 to 1881 he was Atlanta's chief of police, a position he would also hold later in life in Anniston, Alabama. In 1881 he moved to Tuscaloosa, Alabama, and during that same year married his second wife, Linda Spiller. George T. Anderson died on April 4, 1901, at the age of seventy-seven, and was buried in Edgemont Cemetery, Anniston, Alabama.[4]

By the time of the Gettysburg campaign, the 1st Kentucky had been replaced in Anderson's Brigade by the 59th Georgia. The 7th Georgia, formed in May 1861 at Atlanta, Georgia, was led by Colonel William W. White, an antebellum lawyer from Cobb County, Georgia, and had ten companies totaling 400 men. The 8th Georgia had 330 men in ten companies at Gettysburg, and was led by Colonel John R. Towers, a native South Carolinian who was referred to by the entire regiment as "Grand-ma."[5]

The 9th Georgia came to Gettysburg with nine companies totaling 361 men (Company A had been converted into an artillery company in December 1861). The regiment was led by the fifty-year-old Lieutenant Colonel John C. Mounger, a lawyer from Brooks County, Georgia. Mounger would be killed in action at Gettysburg. The smallest regiment in the brigade, containing 328 men, was the 11th Georgia. Its commander, Colonel Francis H. Little, graduated from the University of Georgia in 1861 and began practicing law. At Gettysburg, the twenty-three-year-old Little would be wounded, and command would devolve to Lieutenant Colonel William Luffman, a Mexican War veteran. When he too was wounded, Major Henry D. McDaniel, a participant in the Georgia Secession Convention, took command. The largest regiment in the brigade belonged to the 59th Georgia, which numbered 557 men at Gettysburg. When its colonel, Jack Brown, was wounded, Major Bolivar Hopkins Gee, another member of the Georgia Secession Convention, led the regiment.[6]

Division commander Major General Lafayette McLaws was born at Augusta, Georgia, on January 15, 1821. Of Scottish and French Huguenot descent, McLaws graduated from West Point in 1842 along with James Longstreet. When war broke out with Mexico, he went to Corpus Christi, Texas, and served with General Zachary Taylor's Army of Occupation. He participated in the siege of Monterey and witnessed the surrender of Vera Cruz. Promoted to captain in 1851, Lafayette served under Colonel Albert Sydney Johnston in the 1858 campaign against the Mormons. Following that expedition, Captain McLaws spent the next two years dealing with the Navajo Indians in the Southwest.

After Georgia seceded from the United States on January 19, 1861, McLaws resigned his commission with the United States Army on March 23, 1861, and immediately offered his services to the fledgling Confederacy. He was promptly appointed colonel of the 10th Georgia Infantry Regiment on June 17, 1861. His military talents were quickly recognized and appreciated by his superiors, and he was promoted to brigadier general on September 25, 1861. Within two months, McLaws was commanding a division. He performed well during the Peninsula campaign, especially in the operations around Yorktown, drawing the favorable attention of General

Joseph E. Johnston. Based on Johnston's recommendation, McLaws was promoted to major general on May 23, 1862. His division fought well during the Seven Days' Battles, but missed the Battle of Second Manassas when it was left behind to protect Richmond. In the Maryland campaign, McLaws's performance was poor—he took forty-one hours to march his division from Harper's Ferry to Sharpsburg, barely arriving in time for the battle. Three months later, he redeemed himself at Fredericksburg as his well-fortified men rained down death and destruction upon the attacking Federals. The Georgian's actions in the Chancellorsville campaign once again left much to be desired. On May 3, 1863, his indecision forfeited Lee's chance of defeating Major General Joseph Hooker's VI Corps, isolated near Fredericksburg. In the ensuing reorganization of the Army of Northern Virginia McLaws was passed over for promotion to corps commander. His pride hurt, he requested a transfer, which was denied. Yet when the forty-two-year-old major general rode into Pennsylvania the following month, he was poised to carry out his orders at Gettysburg as well as any other divisional commander, North or South.[7]

The senior brigadier general in McLaws's Division was Joseph Brevard Kershaw. Born at Camden, South Carolina, on January 5, 1822, the future Confederate general had politics and military life in his blood. His father, John, had served in the United States Congress while his mother, Harriet, was the daughter of an aide-de-camp to General Francis Marion in the American Revolutionary War. Joseph B. Kershaw chose law as a profession and was admitted to the South Carolina bar in 1843 at age twenty-one. During the Mexican War he served as a first lieutenant of Company C for the Palmetto Regiment for one year. Returning from Mexico, young Kershaw resumed his law practice and became involved in Palmetto State politics. He served two terms in the South Carolina Legislature and was a supportive member of his state's secession convention in 1860.

In February 1861, Kershaw received a commission in the Confederate service as colonel of the 2nd South Carolina Infantry Regiment, and was present on Morris Island during the bombardment of Fort Sumter. At the First Battle of Manassas, the lawyer-turned-soldier performed very well, leading his men in a well-timed charge across Henry Hill and clearing the position of Federal soldiers. However, he drew the ire of General Pierre Gustave Toutant Beauregard by writing a highly self-congratulatory article for a South Carolina newspaper instead of properly filing a report with Beauregard. In spite of that incident, Kershaw was a good fighter and was promoted to brigadier general on February 13, 1862. At Gettysburg, the forty-one-year-old brigadier's command included the 2nd, 3rd, 7th, 8th, and 15th South Carolina regiments, as well as the 3rd South Carolina Battalion.[8] Kershaw was well respected by his men and his superiors. Lieutenant General James Longstreet would commend him for exhibiting "great gallantry and skill" at Gettysburg.[9]

The men of the 2nd South Carolina, also known as the 2nd Palmetto Regiment, came from Camden, Charleston, and Columbia, as well as from Greenville, Kershaw, Lancaster, Richland, and Sumter Counties. By January 16, 1861, nine of the ten companies had already been filled, and the regiment was mustered into state service on April 9, 1861, three days before the firing on Fort Sumter. Like many Civil War regiments, the 2nd South Carolina had colorful company names, such as Company A, Governor's Guards, and Company C, Columbia Grays.[10]

Upon Kershaw's promotion to brigadier, John Doby Kennedy became colonel of the 2nd South Carolina. Colonel Kennedy was born on January 5, 1840, at Camden, South Carolina. He attended South Carolina College, and was practicing law in Camden at the outbreak of the war. The twenty-three-year-old attorney was Kershaw's youngest regimental commander at Gettysburg, and he led Kershaw's second largest regiment, with 437 men, into Pennsylvania.[11]

When the 3rd South Carolina was organized in Columbia, South Carolina, in April 1861, most of the men came from the five counties of Colleton, Laurens, Newburry, Pickens, and Spartanburg. The company names reflected the fierce state and regional pride of the men.[12]

The men of the 3rd South Carolina elected James Henderson Williams as their first colonel. The forty-seven-year-old Henderson was serving his second term in the South Carolina Legislature, even though he was living on a plantation in Arkansas. Henderson had a solid military background, having fought in the Seminole War and the Mexican War. In the May 1862 reorganization of the army, he was replaced by James Dayton Nance, a lawyer from Newburry, South Carolina, who was born on October 10, 1837. Nance was at home recovering from a wound when the Gettysburg campaign began and did not catch up with his regiment until late in the afternoon of July 3, 1863. In his stead the twenty-seven-year-old Major Robert Clayton Maffett led the 432-man regiment into Pennsylvania.[13]

The 7th South Carolina assembled on April 16, 1861, at the Schutzenplatz, near Charleston, South Carolina. The men in Companies A, B, C, and D were from Abbeville County, South Carolina, while the men of the remaining companies came from Edgefield District, South Carolina. Thomas Glascock Bacon, a forty-nine-year-old veteran of the Seminole War, was elected as colonel. Thirteen months later Bacon declined reelection because of failing health, and David Wyatt Aiken, a thirty-four-year-old former teacher and planter, assumed command of the regiment. When the regiment crossed the Mason-Dixon Line in June 1863 it had 432 men available for combat.[14]

Men from the counties of Chesterfield, Darlington, Marion, and Marlborough joined together in Charleston on April 14, 1861, to form the 8th South Carolina. Red-haired Ellerbe Boggan Crawford Cash, a native North Carolinian who attended South Carolina College, served as the first colonel of the regiment until May 1862. At Gettysburg, the 318-man-strong regiment was led by John Williford Henagan. The forty-year-old Henagan, like Cash, had served in the South Carolina Legislature and had also served as sheriff of Marlboro District.[15]

Kershaw's largest regiment at Gettysburg was the 15th South Carolina, with 476 men. These soldiers, recruited from Fairfield, Kershaw, Lexington, Richland, Union, and Williamsburg Counties, first saw action at Second Manassas, under Colonel William Davie De Saussure. At forty-five years, De Saussure was Kershaw's eldest regimental commander at Gettysburg. He was a graduate of South Carolina College, where he was trained as a lawyer. He also served in the South Carolina Legislature, and had served as a captain in the Mexican War, as well as with the U.S. Army on the western frontier, before the outbreak of the Civil War.[16]

De Saussure was well respected by his peers and subordinates alike. D. Augustus Dickert, the chronicler of Kershaw's Brigade, recalls a letter he received from one of De Saussure's officers:

> In my judgment, he [De Saussure] was the superior of Kershaw's fine set of Colonels, having, from nature, those rare qualities that go to make up the successful war commander, being reticent, observant, far-seeing, quick, decided, of iron will, inspiring confidence in his leadership, cheerful, self-possessed, unaffected by danger, and delighting like a game cock in battle....He understood men, was clear sighted, quick and sound of judgment, and seemed never to be at a loss what to do in emergencies.[17]

De Saussure would be killed in action at Gettysburg during the Wheatfield fighting on July 2, 1863. The papers promoting him to brigadier general remained in the hands of Confederate Secretary of War James Seddon and were never acted upon.

The 3rd South Carolina Battalion, containing seven companies with 215 men at Gettysburg, was Kershaw's smallest unit. Like the 15th South Carolina, the battalion was assigned to Kershaw's Brigade just prior to the Battle of Fredericksburg. Formed in November 1861, the first four companies contained South Carolinians from Laurens County. The additional three companies joined their comrades one month later at White Point along the South Carolina coast. These new men were recruited from Fairfield, Laurens, and Richland Counties.[18]

George Sholter James, first commander of the battalion, was born in Laurens County in 1829. After attending South Carolina College and Erskine College, James served as a lieutenant of artillery in the U.S. Army. He resigned his commission and offered his services to the Confederacy in April 1861, participating in the bombardment of Fort Sumter. James was killed at South Mountain on September 14, 1862, and was replaced by William George Rice. Like many of Kershaw's commanders, Rice had graduated from South Carolina College. When the battalion headed toward Pennsylvania, Rice was on leave of absence. Hurrying back to the action, the thirty-one-year-old lieutenant colonel rejoined his men in Chambersburg, Pennsylvania, on June 28, 1863.[19]

Half of McLaws's Division consisted of brigades whose regiments came from Georgia. Paul Jones Semmes was one of the brigade commanders. Born on June 4, 1815, at Montford's Plantation, Georgia, Semmes attended the University of Virginia. After relocating to Columbus, Georgia, in 1840, the future Confederate brigadier general became a prominent banker and plantation owner. He was also very involved in military affairs and served as captain in the Columbus Guard from 1846 until the Civil War.

During the last two months of 1860, Semmes established headquarters in New York City for the purpose of purchasing military supplies for Georgia, a position to which Governor Joseph Brown had appointed him. When he returned to Georgia on January 3, 1861, his mission was successfully completed, as he purchased more than $93,000 worth of military supplies. Governor Brown offered him a commission as Georgia quartermaster general, which he accepted. Still active in the Columbus Guards, the bold Semmes persuaded president-elect Jefferson Davis to allow the Guards to serve as the honor guard for Davis's inauguration. In May 1861, Semmes resigned his commission with the state militia and was elected as colonel of the 2nd Georgia Infantry. Within a year, he was promoted to brigadier general, to rank from March 11, 1862.[20]

Semmes was well respected by his men. Andrew Jackson McBride of the 10th Georgia remembered his general as follows:

> I doubt if there was a better brigade commander in either army than Paul J. Semmes. Tall, well proportioned, handsome, ruddy complexion, piercing eyes, aquiline nose, his auburn hair just tinging with gray, scrupulously neat in his dress, he was a striking figure and would command attention and respect in any assembly. He was a humble, devoted Christian....When a battle was imminent, General Semmes dressed with extraordinary care, carefully polished boots, spotless linen, elegant uniform, a brilliant sash around his waist and shoulders and a red turban on his head.[21]

Gettysburg would be the last battle in which Paul Semmes would fight—he was mortally wounded on July 2 in the Wheatfield fighting. Ironically, he had a premonition of his demise before crossing north of the Mason-Dixon line. In a letter to a friend on June 23, 1863, he requested that his life insurance policy be renewed:

> If you do not here [*sic*] from me to the contrary renew my policy, it expires the 3rd of July and notify my wife of the renewal. ($863.00) Although it is a heavy tax, still I feel that I ought not to give up the policy under the particular circumstances—God has preserved my health and life up to the present time, but he may see fit to take me from

earth very soon—Indeed having passed through more than the average number of battles unharmed, I ought not to count on much further immunity....Feeling that any battle may be my last one—that is whilst I have no presentment of death—still the peril is so great that I cannot hope to escape much longer....Death has no terror for me.[22]

Semmes's Brigade consisted of the 10th, 50th, 51st, and 53rd Georgia Infantry regiments. The 10th Georgia came to Gettysburg with 322 men, who had been recruited in the Georgia counties of Bibb, Chattahoochee, Clayton, DeKalb, Fayette, Pulaski, Richmond, and Wilcox. It had been organized in June 1861 at Jonesboro, Georgia, and its first commander was Alfred Cumming, a class of 1849 West Point graduate. Cumming resigned his commission in the U.S. Army in January 1861, and began his Confederate service by training Georgia volunteers. He was promoted to brigadier general on October 29, 1862, and was transferred to Lieutenant General John C. Pemberton's Army of Mississippi. While his former comrades were fighting at Gettysburg, Cumming was preparing for the Confederate surrender of Vicksburg.[23]

John B. Weems, a thirty-nine-year-old former merchant, led the 10th Georgia at Gettysburg. Weems came from a militia background, having served as a captain of an Augusta Volunteer Company before the outbreak of the war. Originally commissioned as captain of Company B in the 10th Georgia, Weems was promoted two ranks during the first year of the war. On October 29, 1862, he became colonel of the regiment, leading it until he retired to the Invalid Corps on May 19, 1864.[24]

Soldiers of the 50th Georgia were recruited in Southern Georgia and were organized in the spring of 1862 at Camp Davis. After adopting colorful company names, the regiment was then assigned to Savannah.[25]

Colonel William R. Manning was the first commander of the 50th Georgia, which he led at Gettysburg. Born in 1817, the owner of a large plantation served as a colonel of the militia in the Valdosta, Georgia, area from 1846 until 1852. Gettysburg would prove to be Manning's last large military engagement. At Gettysburg he commanded 321 men, and he resigned from the army on the last day of July 1863.[26]

Similar to the 10th Georgia, the 51st Georgia entered Pennsylvania during the summer of 1863 with 322 men. The regiment was organized in February 1862 of men recruited from the Georgia counties of Baker, Calhoun, Clay, Colquitt, Daugherty, Early, Lee, Miller, Mitchell, Randolph, Terrell, and Washington. Regional pride was reflected in the company names. Company A was also known as the "Early Volunteers" (Early County), and Company B as the "Lee Guards" (Lee County).[27]

William Marion Slaughter led the 51st Georgia from its inception to the spring of 1863. He graduated from the College of William & Mary and worked as a lawyer and planter during the prewar years. On May 1, 1863, Slaughter was mortally wounded at Zoan Church near Chancellorsville and died that same evening. Thirty-three-year-old Lieutenant Colonel Edward Ball, recovering from a wounded heel suffered at Chancellorsville, was promoted and led the 51st Georgia at Gettysburg.[28]

The largest regiment in Semmes's Brigade at Gettysburg was the 53rd Georgia made up of 448 men. It had also been organized in the spring of 1862, with the men coming from Baker, Fayette, Jasper, Mitchell, and Quitman Counties. Leonard T. Doyal, a wealthy lawyer from Griffin, served as the regiment's first colonel. After resigning on October 8, 1862, the popular Doyal was replaced by James Phillip Simms. Simms was born on January 16, 1837, in Covington, Georgia, where he practiced law until the war broke out. Simms led the 53rd Georgia at Gettysburg and was promoted to brigadier general in December 1864.[29]

William Tatum Wofford commanded another brigade of Georgia regiments in McLaws's Division at Gettysburg. Born on June 28, 1824, in Habersham County, Georgia, Wofford graduated from the Gwinnett Manual Labor Institute in 1839. He attended Franklin College in Athens, Georgia, and was admitted to the Georgia bar in 1844. He opened his own law practice in Cassville on March 14, 1845. Two years later, Wofford was a captain of a company of mounted Georgia volunteers in the Mexican War.

After the war, Wofford resumed his life in Cassville as a lawyer and a farmer. He served in the Georgia Legislature from 1849 until 1853, and also owned and edited the *Cassville Standard*, a local newspaper he helped to establish in 1849. When the ominous storm clouds of secession swept across the country in 1860, Wofford's was a voice of moderation in Georgia. He went to the Democratic Convention in Charleston as a Douglas Democrat. When Governor Joseph E. Brown called a state convention to consider secession, Wofford represented his county as an anti-secessionist. When the pro-secessionists carried the convention, Wofford cast his lot with his home state. In March 1861, he was present in Savannah when the Confederate Constitution was ratified by the delegates.

When war broke out, Wofford offered his services to Governor Brown and was immediately elected colonel of the First Regiment of Georgia State Volunteers. This regiment would be mustered into the Army of the Confederate States of America on August 9, 1861, and redesignated as the 18th Georgia. His regiment was brigaded with Hood's Texans, and as senior colonel, he led the brigade at Second Manassas, South Mountain, and Sharpsburg. On January 23, 1863, he learned of his long overdue promotion to brigadier general, to rank from January 17, 1863. His new command was Thomas Reade Rootes Cobb's former brigade and included the 16th, 18th, and 24th Georgia, together with Phillips's Legion and Cobb's Legion.[30]

The 16th Georgia, also known as the "Sallie Twiggs Regiment," contained recruits from Elbert, Gwinnett, Habersham, Hart, Jackson, and Madison Counties. Formed during the first few months of the war, it had Howell Cobb, a most prominent Georgia politician, as its first colonel. Cobb, born on September 7, 1815, was a graduate of the University of Georgia and earned a living as a lawyer. From 1843 to 1851, he served in the U.S. House of Representatives, and served as Speaker of the House from 1849 to 1851. He was governor of Georgia from 1851 to 1855, after which he returned to Congress. He also served as secretary of the treasury in President James Buchanan's administration. Cobb was a strong proponent of secession and was considered by some to be the best choice as first president of the Confederacy. By the end of the war, he was a major general.[31]

Cobb was promoted to brigadier general on February 12, 1862. Command of the 16th Georgia was given to Goode Bryan, a 1834 West Point graduate. At Gettysburg, Bryan was fifty-one years old. He had resigned from the U.S. Army one year after his graduation and spent his prewar years in Georgia and Alabama. When the war with Mexico broke out, Bryan served as major of the 1st Alabama Volunteers. Robert E. Lee recognized Bryan's military talents. Bryan was promoted to brigadier general at the end of the summer of 1863. As Colonel Bryan marched to Gettysburg, he commanded a regiment that was 322 men strong.[32]

Lieutenant Colonel Solon Zachary Ruff led the 321-man-strong 18th Georgia Regiment at Gettysburg. A prewar math teacher at his alma mater (Georgia Military Institute), Ruff was twenty-six years old at the time of the battle. He was promoted to colonel in the fall of 1863, and the commission was backdated to January 17, 1863.[33]

The 24th Georgia, composed of men from Banks, Elbert, Franklin, Gwinnett, Habersham, Hall, Rabun, Towns, and White Counties, was organized during the war's first summer. Eight of the companies adopted the usual fierce nicknames for themselves.[34]

Robert McMillan, an Antrim, Ireland, native, was the regiment's first colonel. He led 322 men at Gettysburg, and at age fifty-eight, he was Wofford's oldest commander during the Pennsylvania campaign. Before the war, McMillan had served as a representative in the Georgia Legislature from Elbert County.[35]

The smallest unit in Wofford's Brigade at Gettysburg was the 226 men of Cobb's Legion, which only had seven infantry companies. These recruits came from Burke, Carroll, Lamar, and Stephens Counties. The unit was organized by Howell Cobb, whose younger brother, Thomas Reade Rootes Cobb, recruited the Legion and was appointed as its first colonel. T. R. R. Cobb, born on April 10, 1823, followed in Howell's footsteps. He graduated from the University of Georgia and began practicing law, earning a well-deserved reputation as a lawyer of the finest quality. He was a strong secessionist and served briefly in the fledgling Confederate Provisional Congress. On November 1, 1862, he was promoted to brigadier general. At the Battle of Fredericksburg he was struck by a minie ball that shattered his thigh and caused him to bleed to death. Cobb's brother-in-law, Lieutenant Colonel Luther Judson Glenn, commanded the Legion at Gettysburg. Glenn had also graduated from the University of Georgia and gone into a law career, as well as serving in the Georgia Secession Convention. He was forty-five years old during the Battle of Gettysburg.[36]

Phillips's Legion was the other unit in Wofford's Brigade. Like Cobb's Legion, it consisted of infantry, cavalry, and artillery companies, but they did not serve as a single command. The infantry companies had been recruited in Habersham, Polk, and Whitfield Counties. Originally containing fifteen companies, there were only nine companies left in the summer of 1863, with 290 men available for duty at Gettysburg. The Legion was commanded during that battle by the thirty-one-year-old Lieutenant Colonel Elihu Stuart Barclay, Jr., a prewar lawyer who had been wounded in the spine and foot and captured at South Mountain in September 1862. His brother, William P. Barclay of the 23rd Georgia, was killed in action on September 17, 1862, at Sharpsburg, Maryland. Elihu was paroled on October 6, 1862, and received promotion to lieutenant colonel December 13, 1862.[37]

Chapter Two

Lee Moves North

In his June 7, 1863, report to President Jefferson Davis, General Robert E. Lee informed Davis of the beginning of the Pennsylvania campaign: "Mr. President: I commenced to draw the army from the vicinity of Fredericksburg on Wednesday morning, June 3. McLaws's Division, of Longstreet's Corps, moved on that day."[1] The immediate destination was Culpeper Court House, and was reached by June 8, 1863.[2] One week later, Longstreet's Corps, including McLaws's Division, left Culpeper Court House, and "advancing along the east side of the Blue Ridge, occupied Ashby's and Snicker's Gaps"[3] with McLaws's brigades posted in Ashby's Gap. On June 21, Longstreet sent a part of McLaws's Division across the Shenandoah River near Ashby's Gap. The following day, Major General James Ewell Brown Stuart "re-established his cavalry, and McLaws' division was withdrawn to the west bank of the Shenandoah before night."[4] On June 24, 1863, Longstreet's Corps was ordered into Maryland, and McLaws's Division crossed the Potomac River on June 25, 1863. McLaws's Division continued north, reaching Chambersburg, Pennsylvania, two days later. There it rested until the morning of June 30, when it moved to Greenwood, arriving there around 2:00 P.M. When the battle opened at Gettysburg on July 1, 1863, McLaws's Division was pushed forward and "reached Marsh Creek, 4 miles from Gettysburg, a little after dark" where they came to rest for the evening.[5]

The march north from the defenses around Fredericksburg
had been eventful. Lee attempted to disguise his true inten-
tions by having Longstreet move east of the Blue Ridge Mountains. When Federal cavalry, supported by infantry, pushed
Stuart's cavalrymen into Ashby's Gap, McLaws was ordered
to hastily move east (his division had already moved into the
Shenandoah Valley, west of the mountains), recross the
Shenandoah, and push back the Union soldiers.

McLaws remembered that June 21, 1863, evening:

> The fording was deep, up to the arm pits of the shorter
> men, but the command went forward with great alacrity,
> and meeting great numbers of the cavalry coming to the
> rear and crossing the river on their horses, while the in-
> fantry were getting wet to take their places. The greeting
> the cavalry received was anything but complimentary. The
> night on the mountain was very uncomfortable, being cold
> and wet.[6]

The men in Kershaw's Brigade were none too happy over
this countermarching. The forced recrossing of the
Shenandoah River was not a welcome task, since the water
was cold and the night air brisk. To make matters worse,
many of the men, believing they were heading into a fight,
left their blankets behind. They faced the cold air with little
other than oil and tent cloths for comfort. Tally Simpson and
a comrade, both of the 3rd South Carolina, tried to stay warm
by lying "upon an oil cloth and covered the best we could,
which was bad enough, and you had better believe we had a
rough time of it."[7]

Blame for the discomfort was leveled at Stuart's Confederate cavalry for failing to hold the gap. Lieutenant Colonel
Franklin Gaillard of the 2nd South Carolina explained his displeasure with the cavalry in a June 28, 1863, letter to his son:

> They now claim in the papers that they [Stuart's cavalry]
> drove them back but we who were there and saw them
> know better. Our Cavalry is very little account and have

very little to boast of. There are more than half of them who are with their horses lamed or sore backed with the wagons. I am glad to see that the newspapers are speaking very severely about them and I hope it will improve them. They have got so now that as soon as a fight begins they think they have nothing to do but go to the rear and let the Infantry do the fighting. Our boys ridicule them very much whenever they pass.[8]

Fortunately for the Confederate invasion plan, the Federals were pushed back and the Southerners continued their march to the Potomac.

The march from Culpeper Court House to the Gap had not been easy. Kershaw reported that the first two days of marching (June 16 and 17) were "excessively hot." Adding to the discomfort of the marching soldiers was the choking, dusty condition of the roads, which was exacerbated by thousands of plodding feet. Also, the stone walls lining the roads radiated the sun's scorching heat onto the soldiers, adding to their misery. Franklin Gaillard acknowledged that problem in a letter home:

> When our troops would be down in a valley, so that no wind could refresh them, with the sun coming down heavily upon their heads, the heat increased by the reflection from the walls, and the dust stifling them so that they could not breathe in pure air, the gallant fellows, many, very many, would turn red in the face from blood rushing to their head and fall to the ground with sun stroke.[9]

On June 17, Kershaw's wagons were sent by way of Front Royal, which alleviated some of the congestion on the roads. Nevertheless, the marching in mid-June was not easy.

By the evening of June 18, 1863, the men in McLaws's Division had reached the Piedmont Depot on the Manassas Gap Railroad. They encamped one mile behind the depot, and gladly rested for the night. The respite was welcomed, with

Major Robert C. Maffett of the 3rd South Carolina recalling that "the march for the past two days was very hot and dusty, many of the men fainting and falling by the way-side."[10]

The next day's marching took the Confederates ten miles farther north, where they ultimately relieved Major General George Pickett's Division on top of the mountain near Ashby's Gap. On June 20, 1863, the advance began later in the afternoon, with the men heading northwest toward Berry's Ford on the Shenandoah River. Recent rain swelled the Shenandoah River and made the crossing difficult. Wading four men abreast, the 3rd South Carolina lost 2,370 rounds of ammunition during the fording. On the Sabbath, June 21, the South Carolinians had to recross the Shenandoah to come to the assistance of Stuart's threatened cavalry at the gap.[11]

Hard marching resumed once again on June 24, 1863, and the soldiers covered nineteen miles from Berry's Ford to Summit Point, on the Harpers Ferry and Winchester Railroad. The following day they covered another twenty-one miles, stopping one mile north of Martinsburg, Virginia. The next day would be memorable when the Georgians and South Carolinians of McLaws's Division crossed the Potomac River into Maryland.[12]

The division marched to the river along the Williamsport Road. It rained while some of the men waded across the Potomac, but the inclement weather did nothing to dampen their spirits or confidence. Tally Simpson wrote to his sister Mary that "Yes, we are again in Maryland, and I trust that ere [sic] we return, the grand object for which we came shall be accomplished, and we may all soon return to our homes in peace."[13] The crossing had a morale-boosting effect. Men yelled and shouted while bands played "Maryland, My Maryland." Reflecting on their fight-free movement into the North, the soldiers sang "All Quiet on the Potomac To-night."[14]

A soldier in Semmes's Brigade remembered very little of the trip from Culpeper Court House to Gettysburg. Yet, he recalled the river crossing vividly:

The river where we crossed was perhaps nearly 200 yards wide and from four to five feet deep. Our passage was characterized by much jollity and merriment. One little bandy-legged fellow of a company in front of ours, who could scarcely keep his nose above the surface, fell down in midstream and lost his gun, and many other mishaps of more or less seriousness befell the unlucky ones on the way. All of which seemed, by some law of compensation, to do about as much good in the amusement afforded the fortunate ones as harm in the discomfiture and dejection of the unfortunate.[15]

Once across the Potomac, McLaws's Division went into camp near Williamsport, Maryland, where the merriment continued. Whiskey was procured in the town, and a gill was distributed to any man desiring it. General McLaws took pride in the fact that the men of his division did not pass up the opportunity to avail themselves of the liquor. Realizing that some of his men may have had their spirits raised a bit too high by the alcohol, McLaws directed that his aide-de-camp persuade the owner of a building in town to remove a U.S. flag flying from its upper story, lest the Confederate soldiers take umbrage and storm the building.[16]

Now on Northern soil, the Confederate soldiers were required to comport themselves with dignity and honor. On June 21, 1863, Robert E. Lee issued his General Order No. 72, outlining how his invading army should act. These orders provided for the proper procurement of supplies from the countryside. Individuals were prohibited from taking, injuring, or damaging any private property. Only designated officers from the commissary, quartermasters, ordnance, and medical departments were allowed to make the necessary requisitions from local authorities or inhabitants. Receipts were to be given for all materials, and the Confederates were required to pay market prices for the supplies. In the event that requisitions were refused "the supplies required will be taken from the nearest inhabitants so refusing, by the order and under the directions of the respective chiefs of the departments named."[17]

On its face, General Order No. 72 appeared to be designed to prevent pillaging of the Northern countryside, and to a small degree this was true. Lee's real intention, however, was to make sure that the vast bounty of supplies was systematically procured and distributed among his entire army for the benefit of all. The manner in which this objective was carried out varied from brigade to brigade.[18]

In Kershaw's Brigade, Tally Simpson adhered to Lee's orders. Yet, he observed that

> This whole country is frightened almost to death. They won't take our money, but for fear that our boys will kill them, they give away what they can spare. The most of the soldiers seem to harbor a terrific spirit of revenge and steal and pillage in the most sinful manner. They take poultry, hogs, vegetables, fruit, honey, and any and everything they can lay their hands upon.[19]

Simpson believed that most of the destruction was carried out by soldiers from Alabama, Mississippi, Louisiana, and Texas in response to the depredations committed by forces under Major General Benjamin Butler in New Orleans and Major General Robert Milroy in Winchester, Virginia. He did note that on the evening of June 27, 1863, "Wofford's Brig[ade] of this div[ision] stole so much that they could not carry what rations they drew from the commissary."[20]

Franklin Gaillard experienced similar reactions with his regiment. In his June 28, 1863, letter to his son he stated:

> Things are very cheap here in their stores but they will not take our money and Gen. Lee has issued very stringent orders about private property. He is very right for our Army would soon become demoralized if they were allowed to do as many of them would like to. Many of them think it very hard that they should not be allowed to treat

them as their soldiers treated our people. But we must not imitate the Yankees in their mean acts.[21]

On the day after his men crossed the Potomac and had their fill of whiskey, Lafayette McLaws had his division back on the roads heading north to Pennsylvania. His men marched twenty-two miles on June 27, 1863, passing through Hagerstown, Maryland, and Middleburg and Greencastle, Pennsylvania, before finally encamping five miles southwest of Chambersburg. The local citizenry came out to see the invaders, making little effort to conceal their displeasure. L. L. Cochran, a member of Company E, 10th Georgia, remembered the inhabitants of Hagerstown and Greencastle

> ...crowded themselves upon the sidewalks of our route with as much apparent curiosity as if we had been orangoutangs [*sic*] or baboons. We were clad in garments very much damaged by hard usage, and while passing through Greencastle, some remark was overheard reflecting upon our personal appearance, to which Henry Daniel, our wag, replied: "We don't put on our best clothes when we go out to kill hogs."[22]

Gaillard thought,

> It is very funny to pass through these Yankee towns to see the long sour faces the people put on. The girls some of them wear little United States flags. Others more indecent hold their noses and make faces. Our men go on and pay no attention to them. They only laugh at them when they make themselves ridiculous.[23]

On June 28, McLaws had his brigades march through Chambersburg and go into camp one mile east of the town. They remained here until June 30, when they marched another five miles east to Fayetteville. While resting around Chambersburg, a detail from the 3rd South Carolina occupied themselves by tearing up and burning the railroad.[24]

The rest of McLaws's Division used the two-day
Chambersburg respite to relax and ready themselves for what
the future would bring. The men happily feasted on Pennsylvania poultry. They also continued to enjoy other impressed
provisions from around the area. Marcus Green of Wofford's
Brigade wrote in his diary, "I got plenty of good brandy and
chickens, butter, loaf, bread, cherry last night."[25] Another
member of the brigade enjoyed reviewing Thaddeus Stevens's
Caledonia Iron Works, which had been destroyed a few days
earlier by Lieutenant General Richard Ewell's men.[26]

Early on the morning of July 1, 1863, the van of Major
General Henry Heth's Division of Lieutenant General Ambrose
Powell Hill's Third Corps engaged dismounted cavalrymen of
Brigadier General John Buford's First Division, and the Battle
of Gettysburg began. Lee, acting upon information supplied
to James Longstreet by a spy named Henry T. Harrison, had
begun consolidating his widespread army on June 29, 1863.
While the fighting raged on the outskirts of Gettysburg
throughout the day, McLaws attempted to move his division
eastward. This would prove to be a time-consuming task.

McLaws had his division ranged along the Chambersburg
Pike by 8:00 A.M. on that first day of July 1863. However, before he was allowed to place his men in motion, he received
orders to permit Major General Edward Johnson's Division of
Ewell's Second Corps to proceed first. When the last of
Johnson's infantrymen had passed, McLaws was again denied
access to the road, this time by Ewell's wagon train. The four-
teen-mile-long train finally finished passing around 4:00 P.M.[27]

McLaws's men kept active while they waited to move that
first day of July 1863. Wofford's Georgians spent the morning
cooking three days' worth of rations. Private John Coxe, Company B, 2nd South Carolina, and his comrades "Passed the
forenoon of the 1st of July in cooking, eating, and drying our
wet blankets."[28] In mid-afternoon his regiment and the rest of
Kershaw's Brigade marched rapidly for two hours, arriving at

the western base of South Mountain. Here they came to a halt, as Ewell's wagon train continued to clog the pike.[29]

The march of McLaws's Division through Cashtown Gap in South Mountain and on toward Gettysburg began in earnest shortly after 4:00 P.M. The men witnessed the backwash of battle, as the wounded returned from the fighting up ahead. Then, too, the sound of artillery filled their ears. Due to the lateness of the hour they realized that it would not be until the following day that they would engage the enemy. Nonetheless, they pushed forward in anticipation, ultimately bivouacking after two o'clock on the morning of July 2, 1863, near Marsh Creek.[30]

By the time McLaws and his brigades encamped near Gettysburg early on July 2, 1863, one-third of the pivotal battle had been fought. As the fighting came to a close on July 1, Lee's top lieutenant, James Longstreet, tried to convince his commander to alter his plans. Longstreet desired a movement by the Confederates around the left of the Federal army. That maneuver would interpose the Army of Northern Virginia between Washington, D.C. and the Army of the Potomac. Such a crisis would require Meade to attack Lee at a defensive position chosen by the Southern chieftain. Lee would have none of Longstreet's suggestion. He emphatically told his corps commander that "if the enemy is there tomorrow, we must attack him."[31]

The march northward into Pennsylvania had not been without hardship for Anderson's Georgians. On June 21, 1863, Private John A. Everett of the 59th Georgia wrote his mother that

> We have bin marching verry hard for 1 week we would march from 20 to 25 miles a day and it was the warmest wether that I Ever Saw in my life thair was Several of our Div dide on the road I fell in the road and was left but I Soon got Over it and went on after my Regt it was a hard march but it was obliged to keep Oald Hooker from Whiping us.[32]

In spite of the hardships, the men were confident. Private Samuel Brewer of Company I, 8th Georgia, recalled that "All the Army impose the utmost confidence in our hero (Genr'l R. E. Lee), for what ever he says must be done, [and it] is done with alacrity nothing doubting."[33]

By June 30, 1863, the brigade had reached Greenwood, Pennsylvania, and at 2:00 P.M. the following day it set out with the rest of Hood's Division on a forced march to Gettysburg, a distance of twenty-four miles. Ten hours later the soldiers rested for four hours at Marsh Creek, then resumed the march to Seminary Ridge, arriving before sunup on the morning of July 2.

While resting with the division along the crest of Seminary Ridge, the Georgians could plainly see the Federal troops in position on Cemetery Ridge and Cemetery Hill. Soon after sunrise, Robert E. Lee passed by the position on his horse. Captain George Hillyer, Company C, 9th Georgia, fondly recalled the words of a fellow comrade upon seeing Lee, "Boys, there are ten thousand men sitting on that horse."[34]

Having made up his mind to fight it out at Gettysburg, Robert E. Lee was up early on July 2, 1863. He met with several of his subordinates near his headquarters on Seminary Ridge. Longstreet met with his commander once again before sunrise. They were joined by Generals A. P. Hill, John Bell Hood, and Henry Heth. Lee developed his plans during that time, focusing on attacking the Federal left with Longstreet's First Corps. Hood remembered Lee's appearance that morning as having his "coat buttoned to the throat, sabre-belt buckled round the waist, and field glasses pending at his side.... He seemed full of hope, yet, at times, buried in deep thought."[35]

Lee had sent Samuel R. Johnston, his captain of engineers, on a reconnaissance mission earlier that morning to find the enemy's left flank. The captain had been with Lee long enough to know that he should be as thorough as possible in order "to consider every contingency which might arise."[36] Johnston left Lee's headquarters and began his mission around

4:00 A.M., taking only three or four men with him. Johnston had learned the art of reconnaissance from Lee himself, as Lee had stated to him that "while in Mexico he could get nearer the enemy and do more, with a few men than with many."[37] Johnston found that to be true in every instance. When Johnston returned from his mission after sunrise, he found Lee sitting on a fallen tree and Longstreet and Hill with him. He reported his findings to Lee, sketching the route he had taken on Lee's map of the area. However, the indication that he had gotten all the way to the Round Tops without encountering enemy troops must be viewed skeptically. If he had reached the Round Tops, there were enough Federal soldiers in that area that he would have had to observe them and include their presence in his report. Thus, it is probable that Lee's second day plans were based on mistaken reconnaissance information.

Longstreet had ordered McLaws to march forward from Marsh Creek to Seminary Ridge early in the morning. Kershaw's Brigade was in the lead, leaving camp around sunrise. The men had been up since 4:00 A.M., but they could not access the road since Ewell's trains were moving toward Gettysburg ahead of them. When Kershaw's regiments finally began their march, they pressed on until they reached the high ground on the eastern side of Herr Ridge near Gettysburg. Here they moved to the right of the Third Corps, coming to a halt about five hundred yards northwest of the Black Horse Tavern. They remained there until noon, when they received orders to move to the southern end of the battlefield.[38]

McLaws reached his destination at about the same time that Captain Johnston returned from his reconnaissance. The Georgian immediately reported to Lee and Longstreet, finding them at the fallen tree near the Seminary. Lee then indicated on the topographical map where he wished McLaws to place his division. The commander placed a line on the map perpendicular to the Emmitsburg Road, near its intersection with the Wheatfield Road, and told McLaws he wanted him to get there without being detected. McLaws requested that he be permitted to reconnoiter the area. Lee advised him that Johnston had already done so. At that point Longstreet interrupted, pointed to the map, and told McLaws to place his division in a different alignment. Lee directly countermanded Longstreet by replying, "No, General, I wish it placed just the opposite." McLaws returned to his division and awaited the arrival of Captain Johnston and orders to proceed.[39]

The now famous countermarch conducted by McLaws's and Hood's divisions of Longstreet's Corps began about an hour after midday on July 2. Captain Johnston presented himself to McLaws and informed him that he was to conduct him on the march. The two men rode to the head of the column, with Kershaw's Brigade being the lead unit. The two divisions left their positions along Herr Ridge and proceeded westerly toward a road running parallel with Marsh Creek. When they reached that road, they turned left and headed in a southerly direction toward the Black Horse Tavern. They passed the tavern, crossed the Fairfield Road, and continued in a southeasterly direction on a road that went to Pitzer's Schoolhouse. Soon they came to a rise in the road and the column came to a halt. McLaws and Johnston immediately realized that if they continued over the hill they would come into plain view of the Federal signal station posted on Little Round Top.[40]

While the troops waited in place, the divisional commander and the engineer searched for another way to proceed without being detected. Their search proved fruitless. McLaws returned to his command in a foul mood, with one Confederate soldier remembering that McLaws was "saying things I would not like to teach my grandson...to repeat."[41]

There was a simple route that had already been traveled by Confederate soldiers earlier that day, yet for some unknown reason McLaws, Kershaw, and Longstreet did not take it. Certainly the path must have been visible to the Southern generals, since Longstreet's artillery under the command of Colonel Edward Porter Alexander had taken it. The young artillerist had been ordered to move his field pieces into position to support the infantry assault against the Federal left that afternoon. Leading his battalions from Herr Ridge, he preceded the infantry division, passed the Black Horse Tavern, and then continued west along Herr Ridge and reached the Pitzer Schoolhouse just before noon. Once his men passed the Black Horse Tavern, Alexander recalled that they took a road

> which at one point passed over a high bare place where it was in full view of the Federal signal station [on Little Round Top]. But I avoided that part of the road by turning out to the left, and going through the fields and hollows, and getting back to the road again a quarter mile or so beyond.[42]

After arriving in position, Alexander awaited the infantry columns of McLaws and Hood. When no infantrymen appeared, Alexander rode back along the route he had traveled, and found the infantry column halted at the same point where the artillery column had pulled off the road to escape detection from the signal station on Little Round Top. Alexander tried to convince the officers at the head of the column to take the same route that his artillery had taken, but the officers were without authority to do so. McLaws and Longstreet had decided to take a different route, adding up to two hours onto their march.[43]

When McLaws and Johnston returned from their cursory reconnaissance, they met Longstreet. They took him to the crest of the hill to show him why they could not proceed along that road. In answer to Longstreet's query on the best route to proceed, McLaws responded that they would have to countermarch. This would prove troublesome though, since Hood's Division had pressed into the rear of McLaws's column. Longstreet approached McLaws to remedy the situation, stating

> General, there is so much confusion, owing to Hood's division being mixed up with yours, suppose you let them countermarch first and lead in the attack.

[McLaws] replied: General, as I started in the lead,
let me continue to do so and he replied, then go on, and
rode off.[44]

This decision caused a good deal of delay, since Hood's men
had to move aside while McLaws's men retraced their march.
Rather than simply turning his division around and letting a
different brigade lead the way, McLaws turned his troops inside out, enabling Kershaw's Brigade to maintain its position
at the head of the column. This maneuver also required men
to wait by the wayside as the South Carolinians retraced their
steps. The marching and countermarching were not easily
accomplished. Ditches and fences had to be crossed, compound-
ing the problems caused by the rough terrain. The fits and
starts necessitated by the reversal of the divisions and brigades added to the difficulties.[45]

There was at least one moment of levity during the afternoon. An ornately dressed Confederate general with shoulder
length golden curls rode by the 3rd South Carolina. A man in
Company D, not realizing the rank of the rider, called out,
"Say, Mister, come right down out of that hair."[46] The insulted
general wheeled his mount and demanded the identity of the
man who insulted him. When nobody came forward, the angry general rode off. By now the South Carolinian realized
whom he had insulted. Yet, he could not resist firing off a
parting insult, "Say, Mister, don't get so mad about it. I thought
you were some d—m— wagon master."[47]

Once the column had been properly untangled, the march
became easier. After returning almost to their starting point
on Herr Ridge, the Southerners gained the Fairfield Road and
followed it northeasterly until they reached the road running
parallel to Willoughby Run. They took this road south, following it past the Dickson, Culp, Plank, and Felix homesteads,
and ultimately arrived at Pitzer's Schoolhouse and the
Millerstown Road. The road was flat but the fences alongside
of it did not permit enough room for normal marching order,
requiring files to be broken up.[48]

When McLaws's men reached Pitzer's Schoolhouse, Longstreet rode up to his divisional commander to discuss tactics for the ensuing engagement. McLaws was unsure as to how the enemy was posted in front of him, and Longstreet assured him that he would be entirely on the Federals' flank. If that were the case, McLaws advised his old classmate, then he would "continue my march in columns of companies, and after arriving on the flank as far as is necessary will face to the left and march on the enemy."[49] This satisfied Longstreet, and he rode away. Of course, the Confederates were not on their enemy's flank. In fact, Union soldiers were arrayed in battle line in front of them, stretching southward as far as Devil's Den.

Chapter Three

Deploying for a Fight

General Lee's battle plans for the second day's fight at Gettysburg were about to unfold, as the marching finally came to a conclusion. During the march that afternoon, Kershaw's Brigade was in the lead, followed by the brigades of William Barksdale, Paul Semmes, and William Wofford. Having passed Pitzer's Schoolhouse, Kershaw's South Carolinians continued east along the Millerstown Road, on the western slope of Seminary Ridge. They crested the ridge at 3:00 P.M., and came into plain view of the Federals posted some six hundred yards away in the Peach Orchard. Kershaw immediately sent forward a skirmish line to encounter the Union skirmishers posted near the Emmitsburg Road. He then moved his men to the right, positioning them in battle line behind a stone wall. The right flank of the brigade was posted near the Philip Snyder house, with the left flank resting near the James Flaharty farmhouse on the south side of Millerstown Road. The regiments were aligned, from right to left: 15th, 7th, 3rd South Carolina, 3rd South Carolina Battalion, and the 8th South Carolina.[1]

The next brigade to deploy was William Barksdale's. The Mississippians moved to the north of the Millerstown Road and took up their position in Pitzer's Woods. The brigade was behind Captain George V. Moody's Madison (Louisiana) Artillery battery. While Barksdale's men were filing into line, McLaws rode back past Pitzer's Schoolhouse to quicken the pace of his remaining brigades. Semmes's Georgians hurried forward and took up a position two hundred yards behind Kershaw's Brigade. The regiments were posted from right to left with the 53rd, 51st, 50th, and 10th Georgia. Wofford's Brigade filed into Pitzer's Woods north of the Millerstown Road and took up a position 150 yards behind Barksdale's Brigade. John Bachelder's map for July 2, 1863, places Wofford's regiments from right to left as follows: 16th, 18th, 24th Georgia, Cobb's Legion, and Phillips's Legion. Gettysburg historian Harry Pfanz points out that Bachelder's sources for this alignment are unknown. However, in an article in the August 5, 1863, *Richmond Daily Enquirer*, a member of Wofford's Brigade placed the brigade with the 3rd Georgia sharpshooters out front, the 18th Georgia on the right, followed to the left by the 24th Georgia, 16th Georgia, Cobb's Legion, and Phillips's Legion. That would have been their customary alignment.[2]

Lee's battle plan for July 2 called for Hood's Division, followed by McLaws's Division, to strike the Federals' front. McLaws's brigades were forced to wait from thirty to sixty minutes before the fighting began, while Hood's Division marched behind them and farther south into Biesecker's Woods.

Anderson's Brigade arrived into a position across from the Emmitsburg Road in the Biesecker Woods, at approximately 3:00 P.M. Hood's Division straddled the Emmitsburg Road once it was in position, with the four brigades placed into two lines. Brigadier General Evander Law's Brigade of five Alabama regiments occupied the far right of the first line, with Brigadier General Jerome B. Robertson's Brigade, consisting of the 3rd Arkansas, 1st Texas, 4th Texas, and 5th Texas, on the left of the first line. Approximately two hundred yards behind this first line, Brigadier General Henry L. Benning placed his brigade of four Georgia regiments (2nd, 15th, 17th, & 20th Georgia) on the right and Anderson's Brigade on the left. Anderson's Georgians were placed in line, left to right, as follows: 9th, 8th, 11th, and 59th Georgia. Colonel William W. White's 7th Georgia had been detached to guard

Hood's right flank from Federal cavalry threats. The regiment took up a position near the Kern house, located half a mile down the Emmitsburg Road, south of the main Confederate line. The regiment would guard that position for the remainder of the day, and deprive Anderson of four hundred men in the ensuing battle in the Wheatfield.[3]

While waiting for the battle to be joined, Joseph Kershaw got a good look at what was in his front. He described it as follows:

> In my center-front was a stone farm-house (supposed to be Rose's), with a barn also of stone. These buildings were about five hundred yards from our position, and on a line with the crest of the Peach Orchard hill....Behind Rose's was a morass, and, on the right of that, a stone wall running parallel with our line, some two hundred yards from Rose's. Beyond the morass was a stony hill, covered with heavy timber and thick undergrowth, interspersed with boulders and large fragments of rock, extending some distance toward the Federal main line, and in the direction of Round Top....Beyond the stone wall last mentioned, and to the right of the stony hill, was a dense forest extending far to the right. From the morass a small stream ran into this wood and along the base of the mountain. Between the stony hill and the forest was an interval of about one hundred yards, only sparsely covered with a scrubby undergrowth, through which a narrow road led in the direction of the mountain. Looking down this road from Rose's a large Wheat-field was seen.[4]

What of the Wheatfield itself? It is located north of Devil's Den and southeast of the Peach Orchard. The field is bordered on the southeast by Houck's Ridge and on the northwest by Stony Hill. The Wheatfield Road divided the northeastern portion of the Wheatfield from the southern edge of Trostle's Woods. A stone wall bordered the southern portion of the Wheatfield and Rose's Woods. A rail fence ran perpendicular from the right end of the stone wall and extended northwest toward Stony Hill. The ground to the northwest of the fence and wall was low, marshy, and covered by a growth of alders. The topography of the Wheatfield was such that the high ground was located at the northwest portion of the field, and the field sloped down to the stone wall.

Arrayed in battle line across the field from Hood's and McLaws's Divisions was the III Corps of the Army of the Potomac, under the command of Major General Daniel E. Sickles. That the Federal soldiers were posted that far west (approximately three-fourths of a mile) from Cemetery Ridge gave rise to a major controversy which continues to rage to this date. The Meade-Sickles Controversy focuses on Sickles's decision to move his division off Cemetery Ridge to its positions along Emmitsburg Road, the Peach Orchard, the Wheatfield, and Devil's Den.

Daniel Sickles was born in New York City on October 20, 1819. He chose the law for his profession, and politics as his avocation. His skills at both quickly positioned him as a bright light in the Tammany Hall political scene. At the age of thirty-eight he was elected to the U.S. House of Representatives, where he served for two terms from 1857 to 1861. When the war erupted, Sickles raised an entire brigade in his inimitable style, offered his services, and entered the war as a brigadier general. He was given command of the Excelsior Brigade from New York (the one he had formed), and fought well during the Peninsula and Maryland campaigns. A promotion to major general, ranking from November 29, 1862, was obtained when his friend Joseph Hooker was placed in charge of the Army of the Potomac. Sickles was given command of the III Corps.[5]

On the morning of July 2 Sickles and his two divisions were positioned on Cemetery Ridge. The left flank of Major General Winfield Scott Hancock's II Corps was on Sickles's right, while the left of the III Corps extended near Little Round Top. However, as the morning hours wore on, Sickles became increasingly concerned with the vulnerability of his assigned position. He felt that the higher ground to his front at the Peach Orchard and along the Emmitsburg Road offered a more defensible position, in part because it afforded a better position for his artillery.

To quell some of his uneasiness, Sickles ordered a scouting party into Biesecker's Woods, seven hundred yards west of the Emmitsburg Road. Accordingly, four companies of Colonel Hiram Berdan's 1st U.S. Sharpshooters (Companies D, E, F, and I) reinforced by the 3rd Maine, proceeded into the woods around noon. Moving north along Seminary Ridge, they encountered elements of Brigadier General Cadmus Wilcox's Brigade in Pitzer's Woods. Soon the small scouting force (approximately three hundred men) engaged the 11th Alabama. The firefight was quickly joined by the 8th Alabama as well as the 10th Alabama. After fifteen to twenty minutes of spirited action, Berdan's force was compelled to retreat to the Federal skirmish line.[6]

The reports from Sickles's sharpshooters confirmed his fears of enemy activity in his front, and he ordered his corps forward off its Cemetery Ridge line. This move was made without authorization from Meade and would prove to become one of the enduring controversies of the Battle of Gettysburg. Sickles would spend the rest of his life defending his move to the Peach Orchard. His motives were, for the most part, purely self-aggrandizement. In moving his corps forward, Sickles created a salient that Longstreet's divisions would viciously attack. Meade, forced to shore up his left flank, had to funnel reinforcements into the breach from the II Corps and V Corps. For his part, Sickles never passed up an opportunity to defend his motives while at the same time attacking Meade's generalship during the battle.[7]

The III Corps's movement off Cemetery Ridge did in fact create a salient angle in the Federal line. Union artillery was placed along the position in an effort to shore up Sickles's resistance. Lieutenant John K. Bucklyn's Company E, 1st Rhode Island Light Artillery was located to the right of the Federal position and faced west along the Emmitsburg Road. Lieutenant Benjamin Freeborn's section of two Napoleons was positioned between the Wentz buildings and the Sherfy house on the western side of the Emmitsburg Road. The right section (two Napoleons) of Captain Nelson Ames's Company G, 1st New York Light Artillery was posted facing west at the northeast corner of the Emmitsburg Road/Wheatfield Road intersection. Ames's remaining four Napoleons faced southwest along the Wheatfield Road. To the immediate left of Ames, facing southwest in the Peach Orchard, was Captain James Thompson's Pennsylvania Light, Companies C and F, with their six three-inch ordnance rifles. Continuing easterly along the Wheatfield Road, Captain Patrick Hart positioned his 15th New York Battery, only four Napoleons, on the north side of the Wheatfield Road. To the left of Hart's battery, Captain A. Judson Clark's 2nd New Jersey Battery was also posted on the north side of the road. Continuing the artillery line in an easterly direction were Captain Charles A. Phillips's Massachusetts Light, 5th Battery (E) and Captain John Bigelow's 9th Massachusetts Light Battery.[8]

There was a gap of approximately three hundred yards between the left of Bigelow's battery and the right of Captain George B. Winslow's 1st New York Light, Battery D. Winslow posted his Napoleons on the high ground at the northern end of the Wheatfield, where they faced southwest toward Rose's Woods. Captain James E. Smith's 4th New York Battery anchored the left of the III Corps line. Smith placed four of his ten-pounder Parrott rifles on Houck's Ridge by Devil's Den. His remaining two pieces were put in the Plum Run Valley, facing the gorge between Devil's Den and Big Round Top.[9]

The infantrymen of the III Corps were interspersed among the artillery positions. Colonel William R. Brewster positioned his Second Brigade of Brigadier General Andrew A. Humphreys's Second Division on the Emmitsburg Road from Trostle's Lane north to the Klingle buildings. To Brewster's left Brigadier General Charles K. Graham stretched his First

Brigade of Major General David B. Birney's First Division from the Wheatfield Road to Trostle's Lane. Colonel P. Regis de Trobriand's Third Brigade of the First Division occupied a portion of the Stony Hill and into the Wheatfield. The far left of the III Corps line was defended by Brigadier General J. H. Hobart Ward's Second Brigade, First Division, and stretched along Houck's Ridge from Devil's Den on the left to the eastern edge of the southern stone wall in the Wheatfield.[10]

The Federal infantry position along the Emmitsburg Road and Peach Orchard came as a surprise to McLaws, who had been informed by Longstreet that he would be on the enemy's flank. While his division waited in place along Seminary Ridge for Hood's Division to file in on the right, McLaws was visited by Longstreet. The corps commander wanted to know why a battery had not been placed in the Millerstown Road. A logical answer was given. "General, if a battery is placed there it will draw the enemy's artillery right among my lines formed for the charge and will of itself be in the way of my charge, and tend to demoralize my men." Longstreet ignored the response, ordered a battery to be placed there, and shortly the Federal artillery began to shell McLaws's men.[11]

By 3:30 P.M. Hood's Division was in place, and he ordered two batteries to open fire on the Federals. Union gunners on Houck's Ridge and around the Peach Orchard returned fire. Enemy shells soon began to fall among Anderson's men. During this barrage Anderson's Brigade received its first casualty. Jackson B. Giles, a courier, was dismounting his horse when a shell tore off his left leg above the knee and threw him ten to fifteen feet in the air. Captain George Hillyer came to his aid, asking the mortally wounded Giles if there was any message he could relay to Giles's parents. The dying private reportedly responded, "Tell them I died for my country."[12] The cannonading, in Anderson's words, created "a very unpleasant condition."[13]

Boulder where Colonel John Wheeler was killed

Courtesy of Adams County Historical Society, Gettysburg, Pa.

View of Rose's Woods, looking south from Stony Hill

Courtesy of Adams County Historical Society, Gettysburg, Pa.

View of Rose buildings, looking southwesterly from Stony Hill

Courtesy of Adams County Historical Society, Gettysburg, Pa.

42

View of Stony Hill, looking east from Rose house

View of Rose farm, looking south from Peach Orchard

Courtesy of Adams County Historical Society, Gettysburg, Pa.

***2nd Andrews Sharpshooters (Massachusetts)
Monument on Stony Hill***

Courtesy of Adams County Historical Society, Gettysburg, Pa.

Zook Monument

Courtesy of Adams County Historical Society, Gettysburg, Pa.

View toward Round Tops, looking southeasterly from Zook Monument

Courtesy of Adams County Historical Society, Gettysburg, Pa.

*View of Zook Monument and Wheatfield Road,
looking south from southern edge of Trostle Woods*

Courtesy of Adams County Historical Society, Gettysburg, Pa.

View of Wheatfield, looking west toward Stony Hill

Courtesy of Adams County Historical Society, Gettysburg, Pa.

Chapter Four

Anderson Attacks the Wheatfield

Before long Evander Law's and Jerome Robertson's brigades advanced against the Federal positions on the Round Tops and Devil's Den. The 4th and 5th Texas, fighting near Little Round Top, needed reinforcements. General Robertson "sent a messenger to Lieutenant General Longstreet for reenforcements, and at the same time sent to Generals Anderson and Benning, urging them to hurry up."[1] The messenger pointed out the position where support was needed. The Georgian acted promptly and ordered his men forward. One private in the 8th Georgia recalled that "the line rose from the grass upon which they were resting and boldly marched to the field."[2] The four Georgia regiments moved quickly and in good order across the Emmitsburg Road and into a wheatfield located north of Slyder's Lane. They were exposed to the fire from Federal artillery for the next three hundred yards and encountered several casualties. Captain Hillyer came upon John Stevens of his regiment, who had been shot:

> The bullet had gone through his clothes, and I had not noticed any wound. I said "What's the matter John?" He didn't tell me he was wounded, or complain of his hurt, but he replied, "Captain, if you will help me over the fence, I will try to go on."[3]

Hillyer, realizing the wound was serious, told his friend to lie down there and the litter corps would care for him. Stevens died at the spot and was buried there before the day was over. Anderson's men continued on at the double-quick pace and obtained protection from the artillery fire by entering Rose's Woods just north of the John Timbers (a free black man) buildings.[4]

Lieutenant Colonel John C. Mounger of the 9th Georgia was another casualty of that advance from the Emmitsburg Road, having been killed while leading his men across the field. Two of his sons, John and Thomas, described his death in a letter written to their mother on July 18, 1863. Tom was with his father when the officer "was shot with a minie ball through the right breast and a grape shot from cannon through the bowels."[5] He died within minutes of his wounding. The loss was doubly hard for his wife, Lucie, for the Moungers had another son, Terrell, who had been mortally wounded at Chancellorsville. In fact Mounger had written to Lucie on May 23, 1863, apprising her of their son's death. It is ironic that the lieutenant colonel had informed his wife that his poor health led to his decision to tender his resignation from the army. In fact his son John found the letter of resignation on his father's corpse and sent it home to his mother. The elder Mounger intended to resign upon returning to Virginia, but never got the opportunity to do so. Mrs. Mounger's grief was not confined to 1863. Her sons John and Thomas survived the ordeal at Gettysburg, but both were killed the following year in the Wilderness.[6]

Having traveled open fields and taken on casualties, the Southerners welcomed the seeming safety of the woods, for the Federal artillery fire was no longer a threat. However, once there, the Georgians of Anderson's Brigade quickly discovered that danger loomed ahead, and heavy fighting would be their lot for the next several hours. Colonel Van H. Manning's 3rd Arkansas, Robertson's far left regiment, was already hotly engaged with the right of Brigadier General J. H. Hobart Ward's brigade posted in the southeastern portion of Rose's Woods along Houck's Ridge. When Manning's men first entered the woods, less than thirty minutes earlier, they ran into Union skirmishers from the 20th Indiana. The men of that regiment had help earlier in the afternoon from the 99th Pennsylvania Regiment, which was posted to the right of the Hoosiers. When Hood's attack began, Ward ordered the Pennsylvanians to the left of his brigade line near Devil's Den, leaving the 20th Indiana to fend for itself.[7]

Captain Charles A. Bell of the 20th Indiana was in charge of the skirmishers. He had his own Company B, along with Company H, with him. Waiting until the 3rd Arkansas was within two hundred yards of his skirmish line, he opened with a destructive volley. Lacking any form of cover and greatly outnumbered, the skirmishers kept up a steady fire as they retreated to the main body of the regiment posted along Houck's Ridge. Here the Hoosiers stopped the initial charge of Manning's men and settled into a heavy firefight.[8]

The 3rd Arkansas reached a ledge of rocks less than one hundred yards from the 20th Indiana's line and was able to effectively challenge the Federal position. Colonel John Wheeler of the Indiana regiment was one of the early casualties. He was shot through the right temple and died instantly while riding his horse behind the line of his men. Soon after, Lieutenant Colonel C. L. Taylor of the 20th Indiana was also wounded, and command of the regiment devolved to Captain Erasmus C. Gilbreath. Gilbreath mounted Wheeler's horse, but the restless animal could not be calmed down. Gilbreath quickly dismounted, and the horse galloped away. The captain then sent a message back to General Ward advising him of Wheeler's death and requesting more ammunition.[9]

The ammunition supply was running low because of the heavy fighting with the 3rd Arkansas. Captain Alfred M. Raphall of Ward's staff advised Gilbreath of the general's instructions: "Hello, Gilbreath, I am sorry Wheeler is gone, but as you are in command General Ward directs me to say that you must hold this line as long as you can using ammunition of the killed and wounded, and when you can stay no longer, fall back toward the small cabin, we passed coming in."[10] Having delivered that message, Raphall was shot in the left arm and had to be helped down from his horse.

The initial attack of the 3rd Arkansas had stalled with the Confederates midway through Rose's Woods. The left of the regiment soon received flanking fire from Companies B and H of the 20th Indiana. The roar of battle was deafening, and Manning's orders could not be heard over the noise. Accordingly, he drew back his left wing piecemeal. The fire from his left was thus contained, and he readied his command for its second push forward. The fire on the left flank resumed, and the Confederates pulled back fifty to seventy-five yards to regroup. Colonel Manning now ordered his men to stretch the line twice its length, to protect the left flank. The Razorbacks advanced a third time, regaining their position at the ledge of rocks. Their persistence and tenacity would soon be rewarded, as support from Anderson's Brigade was on its way.[11]

The 59th Georgia fell into line with the 3rd Arkansas in and among the boulders along the rocky ledge. The Georgians had double-quicked the four hundred yards from the Emmitsburg Road to Rose's Woods and were quite tired upon reaching their comrades facing the 20th Indiana. Yet, there was no time for rest, and the two Confederate regiments advanced on the Federals. Colonel Manning suffered a wound to his nose and forehead during this charge, and turned over command of his regiment to Lieutenant Colonel Robert Samuel Taylor. This first charge by the combined regiments of the 3rd Arkansas and 59th Georgia was not successful in dislodging the Union soldiers posted along Houck's Ridge. Major B. H. Gee of the Georgia regiment attributed the first attempt's failure to the exhausted state of his men.[12]

Once the Southerners regrouped, a second combined attack was made. During this engagement Colonel Jack Brown of the 59th Georgia was wounded. Major Gee had been stunned by the explosion of a shell and was unable to take over for the stricken colonel. Accordingly command of the regiment devolved to the senior surviving officer, Captain Muston G. Bass of Company E. The renewed attack found Captain Gilbreath's men of the 20th Indiana dangerously low on ammunition. Gilbreath ordered his men to fall back. As they did, Southern fire concentrated on the Hoosiers' color guard. Colorbearer Sergeant William J. Horine was felled by a bullet through his right leg. A young corporal quickly seized the fallen flag and carried it safely behind the lines. Gilbreath remembered that the Confederates laughed when the flag fell.[13]

During the advance into Rose's Woods the 11th Georgia was to the left of the 59th Georgia. When the 59th attacked the 20th Indiana, it received flanking fire from the 17th Maine posted along a stone wall running along the southern portion of the Wheatfield. The wall was approximately seventy-five yards from the attacking Georgians. This flanking fire contributed to the repulse of this initial combined attack of the 3rd Arkansas and the 59th Georgia. Fortunately for those men, the soldiers of the 11th Georgia came into supporting position and opened an effective fire upon the Union soldiers along the wall. Major Henry D. McDaniel of the 11th Georgia reported of this early action in the fight for the Wheatfield in his official report:

> The advance made in good order, and, upon reaching the belt of woods in front, a vigorous fire was opened upon the enemy, followed by a vigorous charge, which dislodged them from the woods, the ravine, and from a stone fence running diagonally with the line of battle.[14]

The left center regiment of Anderson's Brigade was the 8th Georgia. These men had a difficult advance. As they swept across the open fields east of the Emmitsburg Road, they suffered many casualties. Once they reached Rose's Woods, the artillery fire was no longer the primary threat. In its stead were Union infantrymen posted at the stone wall in the southern portion of the Wheatfield. These soldiers were, from right to left as the Georgians faced them: the 17th Maine, 115th Pennsylvania, 8th New Jersey, 5th Michigan, and the 110th

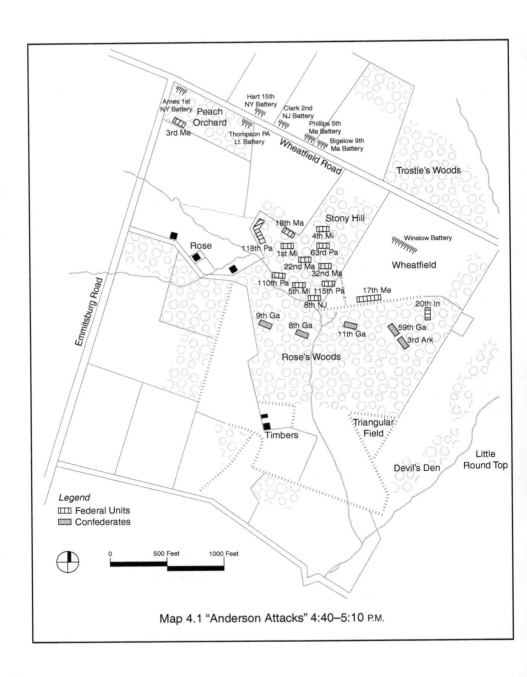

Map 4.1 "Anderson Attacks" 4:40–5:10 P.M.

Pennsylvania. The ground in front of the Federal soldiers was a bog for twenty to thirty yards. The Union soldiers opened fire as the 8th Georgia came into view. Lieutenant J. C. Reid of the 8th Georgia vividly described this initial attack:

> Our lines did not waver under the galling musketry, but came on almost at a run, firing vigorously. I have never read in military history of any soldiers who could deliver such deadly volleys as ours when charging. We were soon ranged along our side of the bog. The fire upon us had slackened; and I saw that ours had been very destructive and that the men in our front were thinking more of shelter by the rocks and trees than of firing.[15]

This was the first of three charges the 8th Georgia made across the boggy terrain around the west branch of Plum Run in Rose's Woods. Several Georgians were killed in the bog. Sergeant Felix H. King was mortally wounded crossing the swampy ground when he got mired waist deep in the muck. As he struggled to keep the colors up he was struck down by musket fire. Another comrade who died in the bog was so deeply embedded in the mire that his body could not even fall over after his death.[16]

The 9th Georgia was the regiment to the left of Anderson's Brigade. It angled toward a ravine nearly due east of the Rose house. The men in the regiment were exposed to a heavy enemy fire from their front and left flank. General Anderson reacted promptly to the crisis and dispatched Lieutenant William A. Tennille, regimental adjutant of the 9th Georgia, to Captain Hillyer with a twofold message. First, since all field and line officers superior in rank to Hillyer had been killed or wounded, Hillyer was informed that command of the regiment devolved upon him. Second, Anderson wished for Hillyer to change the direction of the three companies on the left in order to face the enemy on that flank.

> [Hillyer] gave the command, "Attention three left companies," but the men could not hear my voice, so great, at

the moment, was the roar of musketry and artillery. I
ran to the left of the line, and touching the men on the
back, made the movement mainly by signs; and fronted
the three companies to the left and rear at right angles
to our position.[17]

The flanking fire against the 9th Georgia came from the
110th Pennsylvania, part of de Trobriand's brigade. After leaving Emmitsburg, Maryland, at daybreak with the rest of the
brigade, the 110th Pennsylvania was the rear regiment of the
Union force marching north to Gettysburg. At noon the Pennsylvanians came to a halt near the west side of Little Round
Top. One hour later they were sent out to Sickles's skirmish
line along the Emmitsburg Road. Upon discovering the Confederate advance southward along Seminary Ridge, the regiment was ordered to move by the left flank to a position
northwest of the Rose farm house, where it remained until
3:30 P.M. At that hour de Trobriand had the regiment move
farther east, taking a position on the right of the 5th Michigan, approximately twenty rods (fifty-five yards) south of Stony
Hill. Immediately to their front was the ravine of Rose's Woods,
and to the right front was the wooded bluff of the Rose farm.
The Pennsylvanians held this position for but a short inter-
lude when they were confronted by stampeding cattle and hogs
running away from the attacking Southerners. The first volley fired from the boys of the 110th Pennsylvania and the 9th
Georgia dropped most of those unfortunate animals.[18]

The Pennsylvanians and the men from Michigan held
their position and battled the Confederates. Neither regiment
was very large, and both took heavy casualties. Three companies of the 5th Michigan had been sent out on a skirmish line
around 4:00 P.M., and they took some casualties as Anderson's
Georgians crossed the Emmitsburg Road. Lieutenant Colonel
John Pulford reported that his regiment sustained 105 casualties during the fighting. Private Charles Gardner of the 110th
Pennsylvania was one of the unfortunate soldiers who did not

survive the fighting. A member of the 116th Pennsylvania saw Gardner's body near the Rose house and wrote about it: "One young boy laid outstretched on a large rock with his musket still grasped in his hand, his pale, calm face upturned to the sunny sky, the warm blood still flowing from a hole in his forehead and running in a red stream over the gray stone. The young hero had just given his life for his country."[19] Another member of the regiment died of a gunshot wound to the head as well. Ben H. Barto of Company A ran onto a flat rock and prepared to fire at the enemy, his finger on the trigger, but did not fire. Lieutenant David Copelin ran over to Barto to see what was wrong, and discovered Barto's listless body with a bullet hole through the center of the head. David M. Jones, the lieutenant colonel of the 110th Pennsylvania, was shot through the leg and fell to the ground. Fortunately for him, Major Isaac Rogers was nearby, and he hoisted Jones upon his shoulders, and carried his commanding officer to the top of Stony Hill. He then turned him over to stretcher carriers for treatment. His leg would later be amputated. Jones returned to the fighting and commanded the regiment for the remainder of the battle.[20]

The left three companies of the 9th Georgia continued fighting against the 110th Pennsylvania and the 5th Michigan. The other companies of the Georgia regiment joined with the 8th Georgia to attempt to dislodge the 8th New Jersey and the 115th Pennsylvania from their position between the right of the 17th Maine and the left of the 5th Michigan. The 8th New Jersey and the 115th Pennsylvania were part of Colonel George C. Burling's Third Brigade of Brigadier General Andrew A. Humphreys's Second Division, Third Corps. George C. Burling, a native New Jerseyan, was a solid regimental commander, leading the 6th New Jersey from August 1862. His brigade commander, Brigadier General Gershom Mott, was wounded at Chancellorsville and had not returned to duty by the time the Pennsylvania campaign got underway. Thus Burling, as senior colonel, was given command of the Third

Brigade, Second Division of Sickles's Corps at Gettysburg. His stint as brigade commander ended in August 1863, when Mott returned to active duty.[21]

The position in line of the 8th New Jersey and the 115th Pennsylvania has been a source of controversy since the battle. Major John P. Dunne's July 29, 1863, official report asserts that shortly after 2:00 P.M. the 115th Pennsylvania was "moved off more to the left and placed in position along the edge of a wood in which the enemy's skirmishers and our own were engaged. The front of our line was partly protected by a stone fence."[22] Prior to the 115th Pennsylvania's advance to the stone wall at the southern end of the Wheatfield, Colonel John Ramsey and his 8th New Jersey Regiment arrived there. They immediately took position along the western end of that wall. However, they were soon ordered, presumably by Colonel Burling, to move to their right into an exposed position. The men from New Jersey hastily built rough breastworks from a few rail fences scattered around the area. In front of the regiment "was a thick brush, big timber and rising ground, beyond which was a ravine with a hill on the other side."[23] They were in this position prior to 3:00 P.M., and the 115th Pennsylvania came into line on their left, but there was a gap between the two regiments.

The controversy regarding the position of those two regiments revolves around the postwar recollections of members of the 17th Maine. Lieutenant Colonel Charles B. Merrill's report, dated July 5, 1863, made no mention of any support to the right of the 17th Maine during the Wheatfield fighting. Two decades after the battle Gettysburg historian John B. Bachelder had difficulty placing Burling's two regiments in the Wheatfield and began corresponding with the men from those regiments, as well as the veterans of the 17th Maine, to clarify the situation. Private John Haley of Company I, 17th Maine responded, writing several letters to Bachelder and forwarding two handwritten maps of the area. Haley's recollection was that there was a gap on the right of the 17th Maine, and he had no recollection of the 115th Pennsylvania or the 8th New Jersey being there. Captain George W. Verrill, Company E, 17th Maine, became the most vociferous of the Maine men to downplay the efforts of the New Jerseyans and Pennsylvanians. Verrill maintained that Burling's two regiments were not present at the southern end of the Wheatfield when the 17th Maine held off Anderson's attacks. The issue therefore boils down to whether the 8th New Jersey and the 115th Pennsylvania were to the right of the stone wall in the Wheatfield, and if so, when they were there. Unfortunately, Colonel Burling's official report sheds no light on the controversy. His command was virtually torn apart piecemeal by the III Corps high command, with regiments being sent to different areas of the battlefield and placed under different commanders. His 2nd New Hampshire and 7th New Jersey regiments were detailed to General Graham, the 5th New Jersey to General Humphreys, and the 6th New Jersey to General Ward. Thus, his brigade was scattered all along the III Corps's battlefront. Left without regiments to command, Burling and his staff reported to General Humphreys.[24]

The 115th Pennsylvania was slightly north and to the west of the edge of the stone wall. The men of the 8th New Jersey were to the right of the Pennsylvanians, positioned behind piled rail fences. These two regiments were in place before the 17th Maine moved into the Wheatfield. The men from Maine originally were positioned on the western brow of Stony Hill. As they moved into the Wheatfield to take up a position along the stone wall, they crossed over the Stony Hill and moved diagonally across the field to the wall. This position found their left flank by a large boulder near the right of the 20th Indiana. In arriving there they did not go past the position occupied by Burling's two regiments. With the left flank at the eastern most portion of the wall, the 17th Maine's line would not have stretched along its entire length. Therefore, they would not have linked up with the left of the 115th Pennsylvania. After-battle accounts by the Maine men that asserted Burling's men were not present are not valid. Verrill did recall Pennsylvania troops somewhat to the right and rear of his regiment, but mistakenly took them for the 110th Pennsylvania. As noted earlier, the 110th Pennsylvania was farther west, closer to the Rose farmstead. Major Dunne's assertion that the 115th Pennsylvania was "at the stonewall and in the wheatfield from about 3 o'clock in the afternoon, until [sic] 5 o'clock and did not leave it for one minute" comports with this chronology of being in place before the 17th Maine went to the stone wall.[25]

Dunne's assertion that the 115th Pennsylvania stayed in the Wheatfield long past the 8th New Jersey's withdrawal is not borne out by the casualty rates. Most likely, the 115th Pennsylvania withdrew back across the Wheatfield during the first attack of the 8th and 9th Georgia. Burling's two regiments took the lowest percentage of casualties in the action, with the 8th New Jersey suffering 27.6 percent loss out of its 170 men and the 115th Pennsylvania suffering a rather small 15.9 percent casualty rate among its 151 members. These figures attest to the fact that those regiments did not last long in the fighting before they withdrew. Burling was not present at the time, having gone with the 6th New Jersey to Ward's support, so there was no one to keep them from falling back. They stopped for a short time to lend support to Winslow's battery. After the 115th Pennsylvania withdrew from their initial position, the 8th New Jersey quickly followed, pulling back along the eastern slope of Stony Hill. "As they fell slowly back, their colors become entangled in a tree. The remnant of brave fellows rallied around them with cheers and re-formed to meet the advancing foe. At this point the Eighth was subjected to a severe musketry fire and sustained heavy losses."[26] After they saved the colors, the New Jerseyans completed their withdrawal and left the Wheatfield before the 115th Pennsylvania, who remained near the right flank of Winslow's battery.[27]

The position held by the 8th New Jersey and 115th Pennsylvania was a difficult one to maintain. Daniel Gookin,

Company B, 17th Maine, referred to it in his journal: "The Regts on the right of us had no protection but such as a rail fence afforded, in consequence of which they didn't stand crowding so well as we did, and when the Rebs pressed them closely they gave way and left us exposed to a galling flank fire which no body of men can long endure."[28] The repulse of Burling's men by the 8th and 9th Georgia regiments caused dire problems for the right flank of the 17th Maine. Lieutenant Colonel Merrill responded promptly to the threat. As the Georgians exploited the gap, Merrill decided to refuse three and one-half of the companies on the 17th Maine's right flank along the rail fence running perpendicular to the stone wall. He gave the orders to Lieutenant Charles W. Roberts, the regiment's adjutant, who quickly spread the word to the captains of the companies. During the silver anniversary of the battle, Roberts recalled that "the movement was promptly executed in the face of a severe fire from the enemy in front and upon our flank, but with heavy loss to the regiment, two of the captains and one of the lieutenants receiving mortal wounds and many of the enlisted men falling under the shower of bullets."[29]

The 8th and 9th Georgia soon discovered that their advanced position posed some unanticipated problems. Their left flank was exposed to fire from the 5th Michigan and 110th Pennsylvania, while the refused companies (H, K, and C) of the 17th Maine peppered their right flank. Unable to advance any farther, the left flank assault of Anderson's Brigade stalled.[30]

The 11th Georgia kept the remaining companies of the 17th Maine heavily engaged along the stone wall. The Georgians rushed forward, and the fighting on both sides became desperate. John Haley's memoir was indicative of the fighting spirit of the men from Maine, saying "they [11th Georgia] had not gained the stonewall; nor had we abandoned its friendly shelter. Still our losses were considerable. What theirs were we could not determine. If the enemy was determined to seize this line of defence, it was our determination that he should

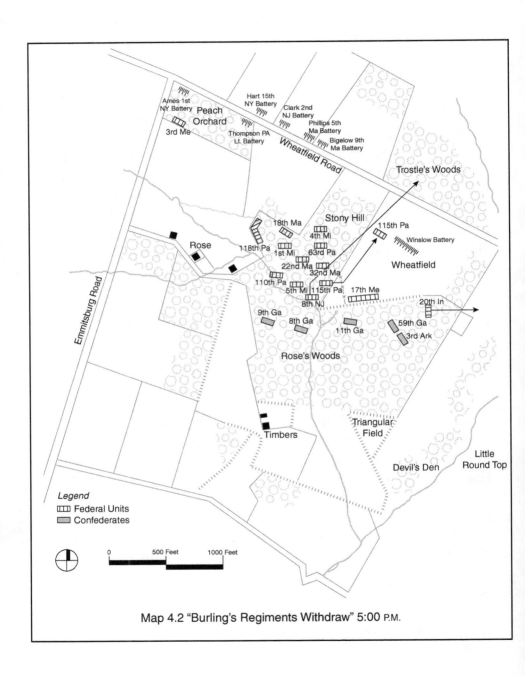

Map 4.2 "Burling's Regiments Withdraw" 5:00 P.M.

only have it by carrying it."[31] The Confederates who attempted to plant their colors on the wall were repulsed, and in the process one of the color guards was captured by Lieutenant Joseph Perry. When the fire grew too deadly, the men of the 11th Georgia were forced to disengage. A short while later, "the gallant prisoner was shown around as a model soldier and sent back under guard."[32]

In spite of the partial success enjoyed by the 8th and 9th Georgia on the left and the 59th Georgia on the right, Anderson's position in Rose's Woods was tenuous. As enemy fire upon his left flank continued, he came forward to confer with Colonel Francis H. Little of the 11th Georgia and ordered Little's regiment to withdraw toward the edge of the woods to regroup. This maneuver was carried out successfully. The left flank regiments fell back as well, and a temporary lull in the fighting occurred around 5:30 P.M. The first phase of Anderson's attack in the Wheatfield ended.[33]

By this time, General Sickles's defensive line quickly began to unravel. Earlier in the afternoon, he moved his III Corps from its assigned position along Cemetery Ridge westward to the Emmitsburg Road. The Second Division, commanded by Brigadier General Andrew A. Humphreys, was posted along the Emmitsburg Road, north of the Wheatfield Road. The First Division, commanded by Major General David B. Birney, was assigned the task of holding the Federal line from the Peach Orchard to the Round Tops. Birney attempted to do so by posting Brigadier General Charles K. Graham's brigade in the Peach Orchard, de Trobriand's brigade on the Stony Hill west of the Wheatfield, and Brigadier General J. H. Hobart Ward's brigade at Devil's Den and Houck's Ridge. To protect the gap between de Trobriand's left and Ward's right, Sickles relied on Captain George T. Winslow's Company D, 1st New York Artillery. Winslow positioned six Napoleons three hundred yards to the north of the stone wall.

Birney reacted to Longstreet's cannonading and Hood's assault by strengthening the left of his line. The 8th New Jersey and 115th Pennsylvania went into position to the west of the stone wall. The 17th Maine moved from the western slope of Stony Hill across the Wheatfield and into position at the stone wall, while the 40th New York was sent to strengthen Ward's brigade. The removal of the 40th New York and 17th Maine from the western slope of Stony Hill left that area vulnerable to any Confederate attack from the west. Birney assured de Trobriand that troops would be filtered into that position shortly, for the French colonel seemed unconcerned about that threat.

The troops filtered into that position belonged to Major General George Sykes's First Division, V Corps, under the command of Brigadier General James Barnes. George Sykes benefitted from the shakeup of the hierarchy of the Army of the Potomac on June 28, 1863. When George Meade was promoted to lead the army, his former position as head of the V Corps was turned over to the forty-one-year old Sykes, a career army man. The Dover, Delaware, native graduated from West Point in 1842 and served with distinction in the Mexican War. He was promoted to major general on November 29, 1862, after he had been leading the Second Division, V Corps since May 1862. Fortunately for the untested corps commander, his command included a division of U.S. Regulars who would perform most admirably on July 2 in the Wheatfield fighting.[34]

James Barnes, born on December 28, 1801, in Boston Massachusetts, was the Union army's oldest divisional commander at Gettysburg. A classmate of Robert E. Lee at West Point, he graduated fifth in the Class of 1829. Unlike Lee, Barnes soon tired of the military life and went to work in the civilian sector in 1836, ultimately becoming superintendent of the Western Railroad. Using his connections in 1861, he received commission as colonel of the 18th Massachusetts. He was promoted to brigadier general on November 29, 1862, and given command of the First Division, V Corps, after Chancellorsville. Gettysburg would be his first combat action at the head of a division, and he would not distinguish himself at all in the fighting.[35]

Barnes's division was near Powers Hill when the artillery opened fire. His three brigades started west along Granite Schoolhouse Lane. With Colonel Strong Vincent's brigade in the lead, followed by Colonel Jacob Sweitzer's and Colonel William Tilton's brigades, the division crossed through the fields north of George Weikert's farmhouse. Soon thereafter, Vincent led his brigade to the summit of Little Round Top, while Sweitzer and Tilton turned southward, swept through Trostle's Woods, crossed Wheatfield Road, and headed south along Stony Hill. William S. Tilton benefitted when Barnes took over as commander of the V Corps's First Division, for the colonel was then given command of that division's First Brigade. A native Bostonian, Tilton was a merchant before the war and volunteered for the 22nd Massachusetts in September 1861. Thirteen months later he was promoted to colonel. His service as an officer was nondescript, and the Wheatfield fight would be the first time he led a brigade into combat. Jacob B. Sweitzer's military record was similar to Tilton's in that his commands were lightly engaged leading up to Gettysburg. A native Pennsylvanian, Sweitzer entered the war on July 4, 1861, as a major with the 33rd Pennsylvania. He was promoted to colonel the following summer, leading his regiment at Antietam in September 1862. He was promoted to brigade command at the end of the following month.[36]

While en route, the men stopped briefly. James Houghton of the 4th Michigan used the opportunity to fill his canteen with water from a nearby ditch. Brushing aside the scum on the top of the water, Houghton smacked the water with his cup to chase away the bugs before filling his canteen. Other members of his regiment followed suit before the Wolverines quickly returned to the march.[37]

Oscar W. West, Company H, 32nd Massachusetts, also had a parched throat. He was denied permission to go to the

Rose branch of the Plum Run Creek in his front to fill his canteen and those of three of his comrades. Not to be denied, West pressed his case further, and was referred to George L. Prescott, the regiment's colonel. Prescott reluctantly agreed, admonishing his thirsty subordinate to "get back just as quickly as you possibly can," an order West gladly followed.[38]

Tilton arrived on Stony Hill before Sweitzer and took up a position facing south along its southern slope. The 22nd Massachusetts (137 men) was on the left, the 1st Michigan (145 men) in the center, and the 118th Pennsylvania (233 men) on the right of the brigade line. The right wing of the Pennsylvania regiment was refused and faced west. The 18th Massachusetts (139 men) was held in reserve, facing southwest, behind the 1st Michigan. To the front and right of Tilton's brigade were the 110th Pennsylvania and 5th Michigan, which extended its line toward the Rose farm house.[39]

The next Federal brigade to go into position belonged to Colonel Sweitzer. He had met with Sykes and Barnes on Stony Hill and received orders to place his brigade (minus the 9th Massachusetts, which had been placed on picket duty near Powers Hill earlier in the day) along Stony Hill. The brigade went into line facing west. The 4th Michigan (342 men) was placed on the right of the brigade line. The 62nd Pennsylvania (426 men) was in the middle, and the 32nd Massachusetts (242 men) was on the left of the brigade position. The Massachusetts men found themselves in an area of low, open ground. Sweitzer reported that both Sykes and Barnes were present on Stony Hill and designated the point where his right flank was to be placed.[40]

This maneuver placed the 32nd Massachusetts to the south, and in front of Tilton's left regiment, the 22nd Massachusetts. Thus, the left flank of the 32nd Massachusetts extended toward the Plum Run ravine in Rose's Woods. To the east and rear of the 32nd Massachusetts was the 8th New Jersey. Sweitzer soon realized the precarious position of this regiment and immediately withdrew the left flank of the 32nd

Massachusetts until the regiment ultimately came into line with Tilton's brigade to the right, and faced south. He had "directed Colonel [George L.] Prescott [32nd Massachusetts] to change his front to the rear, so as to give him the benefit of the elevated ground [the southern slope of Stony Hill] and the cover of the woods, which movement he executed."[41] This movement faced the 32nd Massachusetts in the same southwesterly direction as the rest of Tilton's line, and extended the left of the First Brigade line. Sweitzer then directed the 62nd Pennsylvania and 4th Michigan "to change front to the left, and form lines in the rear of the Thirty-second Massachusetts, to strengthen that position."[42] The two regiments changed front to the left and rear, which brought them into a defense by depth position behind the 32nd Massachusetts. This maneuver placed both V Corps brigades in a position facing southwesterly in the direction of Anderson's attacking Georgians.[43]

The timing of the arrival of Barnes's two brigades on Stony Hill has been difficult to determine because of the paucity of battle accounts dealing with their involvement in the first phase of the Wheatfield fight. They were in place either before or after Anderson's first assault in the Wheatfield. The fact that there are no accounts from any of de Trobriand's or Burling's regiments that mention Tilton's or Sweitzer's men being present support the notion that they were not present during the opening action. In support of the proposition that they saw action from the beginning, both Tilton's and Sweitzer's reports state that they were in line just before the Confederate onslaught. Had they come onto the scene after the first assault, the 32nd Massachusetts would not have been able to take up its initial position extending toward Plum Run without Southern opposition. Additionally, when Anderson's second assault began, it was assisted by Kershaw's Brigade on its left. As time would tell, it was the threat of Kershaw's troops flanking Tilton that caused him to withdraw. Finally, Barnes's three brigades were in motion toward Stony Hill when Colonel Strong Vincent's brigade was intercepted and sent to

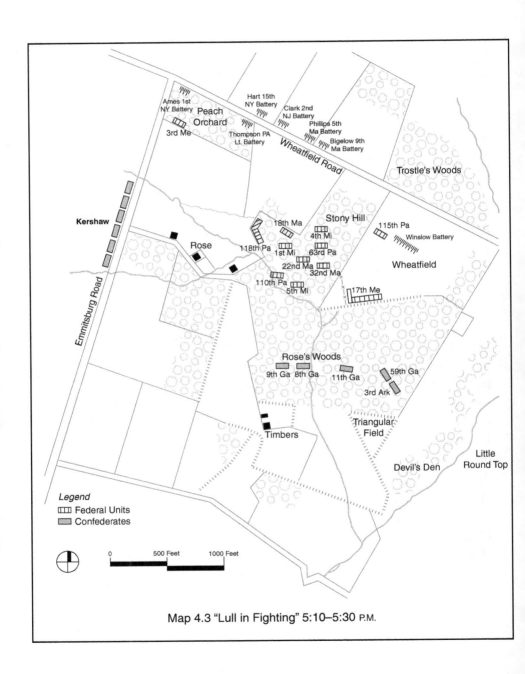

Map 4.3 "Lull in Fighting" 5:10–5:30 P.M.

Little Round Top, arriving there in time to contest Evander Law's Confederate brigade. Tilton and Sweitzer most certainly arrived at Stony Hill at the same time Vincent got to Little Round Top, plenty of time to be there for Anderson's initial assault. If Tilton and Sweitzer came in after the first assault, they would have remained on the field for only a very short time before pulling out, and their casualties do not illustrate such a short stay. Tilton's undersized brigades, totaling only 655 men, suffered a 19.1 percent casualty rate, hardly indicative of a limited appearance on the hill. Sweitzer's brigade had 1,010 men on the hill and suffered a 41.6 percent casualty rate, although most of those losses would occur later that day.[44]

Chapter Five

Kershaw Joins the Fray

The lull after Anderson's first attack enabled both sides to prepare for the coming carnage. Of immediate concern for the 17th Maine men was replenishing their ammunition supply, which had been all but expended in the first attack. The soldiers took ammunition from disabled comrades. When the 11th Georgia color guard prisoner was sent to the rear under guard, the Maine guard was instructed to obtain more ammunition for the regiment. Colonel de Trobriand was on the field attempting to rally his men. When General Birney sent an aide to the Frenchman seeking reinforcements, the colonel demonstrated the severity of the situation by exclaiming, "Tell General Birney that I have not a man left who has not upon his hands all that he can do, and tell him that, far from being able to furnish reinforcements to any one, I shall be in need of them myself in less than a quarter of an hour."[1]

Anderson sought out Colonel W. D. De Saussure's 15th South Carolina Regiment of Brigadier General Joseph B. Kershaw's Brigade for support on his left flank. Anderson arranged for the South Carolinians to aid in the renewed attack against the Federals. While walking toward the right wing of his brigade to further prepare the attack, he was struck down by a minie ball that hit him in the right thigh. The bullet passed through the femoral artery and the bone. Luckily it was not a mortal wound, but it did take him out of the action for the remainder of the battle. He was evacuated to a temporary hospital (one of the Plank family houses) near Black Horse Tavern. Lieutenant Colonel William Luffman of the 11th Georgia, Anderson's old regiment, took over command of the brigade.[2]

The second phase of the Wheatfield fighting began, with Anderson's and Kershaw's brigades threatening the Federal position on Stony Hill. The danger to Tilton's brigade came from the advance of Kershaw's Brigade. The South Carolina general had received orders that he was to attack after receiving a signal from the artillery. The artillery had been engaged in a deadly cannonading with the Federal batteries posted along Emmitsburg Road and Wheatfield Road. The action had been so severe that Edward Porter Alexander, Longstreet's de facto artillery chief at Gettysburg, wrote of the July 2 action, "I don't think there was ever in our war a hotter, harder, sharper artillery afternoon than this."[3]

The prearranged signal for Kershaw to begin the attack was a short respite in artillery fire, followed by the firing of three cannons in rapid succession. Kershaw advised his regimental commanders of the signal and waited for it to be given. After Hood's Division had engaged the enemy, the signal was given, and the South Carolinians started across the open field toward the Emmitsburg Road. Kershaw and his staff were on foot, and Longstreet walked with his brigade commander to the road. As they were approaching the road, Kershaw heard "Barksdale's drum beat the assembly, and knew then that [he] should have no immediate support on [his] left."[4]

The lack of support on his left required Kershaw to alter his attack plans. He had expected Barksdale to advance with him, supporting his left flank. It is probable that the Mississippians failed to do so because of their original position. They were originally positioned among Alexander's artillery along Seminary Ridge, and it was difficult to extricate themselves smoothly and proceed into line. Kershaw's main concern became the Federal infantry and artillery positioned at the rear of the Peach Orchard. He advised his left wing, comprised of the 8th South Carolina, the 3rd South Carolina Battalion, and the 2nd South Carolina, to change direction to the left and attack the Union batteries along the Wheatfield Road. His men carried out their orders: as they passed north of the Rose buildings they wheeled to the left and attacked.[5]

As the left wing of the South Carolinians moved to the left and entered the depression south of the Peach Orchard, the Federal artillerists opened fire. Private John Coxe of the 2nd South Carolina remembered that

> Just as our left struck the depression in the ground every Federal cannon let fly at us with grape. O the awful deathly surging sounds of those little black balls as they flew by us, through us, between our legs, and over us! Many, of course, were struck down, including Captain Pulliam, who was instantly killed. Then the order was given to double-quick, and we were mad and fully determined to take and silence those batteries at once. We had gotten onto the level land of the Federal guns when the next fusillade of grape met us. One of the little black balls passed between my legs. We were now so close to the Federal gunners that they seemed bewildered and were apparently trying to get their guns to the rear.[6]

Although unable to see his left wing's advance on the artillery, Kershaw nonetheless reported the attack being made "in magnificent style."[7] It may have looked magnificent, but the losses among the South Carolinians were ghastly. Solid shot and canister spewed forth from the Federal muzzles. Sergeant William H. Clairville, the chief of piece in Clark's Battery B, 2nd New Jersey, calmly yelled out to his gunner, Corporal Elias H. Timm, "This is the stuff to feed them; feed it to their bellies, Timm; mow them down, Timm."[8]

William Johnson of Company F, 2nd South Carolina, witnessed many of his comrades getting killed and wounded from the murderous fire. In a newspaper article written forty years after the battle, Johnson remembered that "about every other squad which got in it [the depression] was decimated, and I saw that the men about me would be the unfortunate ones."[9] Johnson tried to keep up a steady fire as the advance continued.

The movement by the left wing had its desired effect, as the cannoneers began to fall back from their guns. The South Carolinians were poised to overrun the enemy along the Wheatfield Road when disaster struck. While the right wing of the brigade made its way toward Stony Hill, the center regiment—the 7th South Carolina—lapped the 3rd South Carolina a bit. Kershaw sought to rectify this situation and explained in his official report:

> In order to restore the line of the directing battalion (the Seventh South Carolina), as soon as we reached the cover of the hill, I moved it a few paces by the right flank. Unfortunately, this order given only to Colonel [D. Wyatt] Aiken, was extended along the left of the line, and checked its advance.[10]

As a result, the left wing, which was ready to pounce on the Federal artillery, moved to the right. This enabled the Union soldiers to return to their cannon and renew the firing on the South Carolinians, who were now moving from right to left across the Federals' front. Kershaw lamented that "Hundreds of the bravest and best men of Carolina fell, victims of this fatal blunder."[11]

Undoubtedly one of Kershaw's staff relayed the message, intended only for Colonel Aiken, to the rest of the regiments on the left wing. That the order was obeyed in the face of pending casualties gave testimony to the bravery and dedication of the men. Franklin Gaillard summed it up by indicating that they had to obey:

> supposing that the orders came from Gen. Kershaw, I afterwards learned that it did not. The consequences were fatal. We were, in ten minutes or less time, terribly butchered. A body of infantry to our left opened on us, and as a

voley of grape would strike our line, I saw half a dozen at a time knocked up and flung to the ground like trifles. In about a short space of time we had about half our men killed or wounded. It was the most shocking battle I have ever witnessed. There were familiar forms and faces with parts of their heads shot away, legs shattered, arms torn off, etc.[12]

Several other men in the brigade recalled that fateful afternoon and the destruction wrought by the misguided order to move to the right. Sergeant William T. Shumate of the 2nd South Carolina was anticipating the capture of a battery less than one hundred yards in his front when he and his comrades heard, "in a clear, ringing tone, above the din of conflict, the command, 'By the right flank!'"[13] and they carried out the order. This allowed the enemy to return to their guns and rain down shot and shell upon them.[14]

The 9th Massachusetts Battery, under the command of Captain John Bigelow, contributed to the raking fire against the left wing of Kershaw's Brigade. The South Carolinians were struck by devastating canister volleys that tore holes in their ranks and left many for dead. Some of the Confederates retreated toward the relative safety of the Rose buildings, while most of them moved to the woods on the northern spur of Stony Hill. Once they reached Stony Hill, sharpshooters were sent out to harass the Union artillerymen along Wheatfield Road. The terrain provided cover for the sharpshooters, and their fire was effective. At about 6:00 P.M. the Federal artillery positions became untenable, and Lieutenant Colonel Freeman McGilvery, First Volunteer Brigade artillery commander, ordered the withdrawal of his batteries.[15]

Kershaw's right flank had better success. After his line had been rectified, the 3rd and 7th South Carolina took possession of Stony Hill. They fought Tilton's and Sweitzer's brigades, which were posted at the southern end of Stony Hill. The right wing of Tilton's brigade was closest to Kershaw's attacking men, and the 118th Pennsylvania became hotly engaged with the South Carolinians. One soldier in the Pennsylvania regiment remembered

> ...across the unguarded space [ground from the Rose buildings to Stony Hill] a column of the enemy appeared through the smoke, moving with shout, shriek, curse and yell about to envelop the entire exposed and unprotected right flank of the regiment. They were moving obliquely, loading and firing with deliberation as they advance.[16]

The pressure on the Union position near the Wheatfield intensified. After his first attack stalled, "Tige" Anderson realized he needed support on his left flank. He sought out Colonel William D. De Saussure, commander of the 15th South Carolina of Kershaw's Brigade. The 15th South Carolina had been separated from the rest of its brigade by the Confederate artillery at the time of the initial advance from Biesecker's Woods. Anderson found De Saussure and made the appropriate arrangements for the renewed attack.[17]

Anderson's second attack included three of Kershaw's regiments, the 15th, 7th, and the 3rd South Carolina, which put severe pressure on Tilton's men. John L. Smith of the 118th Pennsylvania wrote to his mother one week after the fighting that

> The Rebs came down the hill in front of us in droves and we opened fire on them very lively. I loaded and fired 15 times. They were so thick that you could shut your eyes and fire and could hit them, and they jumped behind every tree and stump for cover and halted at the edge of the woods.[18]

The 118th Pennsylvania had thrown out a line of skirmishers which were driven back in short order to the regimental line. The Pennsylvanians loaded and fired as quickly as they could. Many of them were so intent in combating the enemy that they did not even avail themselves of the natural defenses (boulders and trees) that marked their position. Captain Francis Donaldson of the 118th Pennsylvania remembered one of his comrades, "like a blazing Vesuvius, standing a yard to two in front of all, begrimed with powder, hatless and shouting as he fired his piece, 'Give them hell boys', and by his extraordinary behavior making himself the most conspicuous object in our line."[19]

The 22nd Massachusetts had also sent out a skirmish line. When they came running back to the main line, the men in the regiment fixed bayonets. The men from Massachusetts placed their cartridges and caps on the ground in front of them, waiting for the inevitable. Soon the Confederates attacked and confusion reigned. John Parker, regimental historian of the 22nd, remembered the clear ringing of the Rose farm bell whenever it was struck by a bullet. He also wrote after the war that

> The green leaves and twigs fell from overhead in a constant shower, clipped by the singing bullets. Indistinct masses of men across the run, with here and there the cross-barred Confederate battle-flag, were now visible.[20]

The right flank of the 118th Pennsylvania bent back to face west, the direction of the attacking South Carolinians.

Colonel Tilton was wary of his position. Although it was a strong position on high ground, he quickly determined that it was untenable. His fears were confirmed when he saw the left flank of Kershaw's Brigade moving toward the woods on the northern end of Stony Hill. Not realizing those regiments were being badly raked by shot and shell, he misinterpreted the maneuver as a flanking movement against his position. His second cause for concern was the retreat of the batteries along Wheatfield Road. Without their support on his right, Tilton's flank would be left unprotected, and he decided the time was at hand to move from that position. He relayed his opinion to his divisional commander, who ordered him to fall back if he was unable to hold the position. When Tilton personally

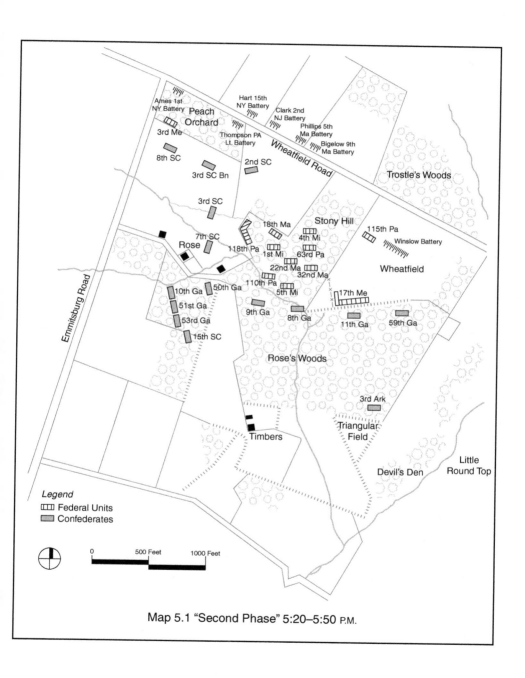

Map 5.1 "Second Phase" 5:20–5:50 P.M.

reconnoitered the situation and saw the South Carolinians approaching, he immediately ordered the withdrawal of his brigade north to a new position in Trostle's Woods to the left and rear of Bigelow's battery.[21]

The decision to pull off Stony Hill was not a popular one with the rank and file of Tilton's brigade. The men in the 118th Pennsylvania had become engaged in a firefight with Kershaw's men. When Tilton's aide approached Lieutenant Colonel James Gwynn to inform him of the order to withdraw, the fighting Pennsylvanians realized what was in store for them. Shouting, "No retreat! No retreat! We're on our own soil,"[22] they sought to dissuade their commander from abandoning the position, but to no avail. Soon Major Charles P. Herring shouted, "Change front to the rear," and the retreat was underway.[23]

Since the impact of the retreat was felt first by the 118th Pennsylvania, its officers sought to maintain good order in the retrograde movement. Captain Francis Donaldson ran to the rear of his company to steady his men. Once there, he was approached by Captain Richard W. Davids of Company G. Davids informed Donaldson that he had been hit in the stomach, and Donaldson urged him to go to the rear for treatment. Before the wounded captain walked twenty steps, he fell into the arms of John L. Smith, who eased him to the ground. Members of Company G came along and carried their captain's corpse from the field.[24]

The Confederates were relentless in their attack upon the Federals on Stony Hill, and they were successfully flanking the 118th Pennsylvania. The regiment could no longer hold the position and began a fighting withdrawal. The 1st Michigan joined the 118th Pennsylvania as they retreated northward along Stony Hill toward Trostle's Woods. The 18th and 22nd Massachusetts moved by the left flank to the rear, passing north on the crest of Stony Hill. In an act of defiance, Captain Lemuel Crocker lingered behind as his comrades in the 118th Pennsylvania withdrew. He indicated to Donaldson that he wanted to determine the size of the enemy force to see what their next move might be. Having satisfied himself of that inquiry, he grabbed Donaldson's pistol, fired two shots at the South Carolinians, and then ran away, followed closely by Donaldson.[25]

While the 118th Pennsylvania defended itself, the men of the 22nd Massachusetts experienced their own threat. Their line was being pressed on both sides by Confederates. When they were completely flanked, the order was given to change front to the rear, and they began their retreat, arriving at Trostle's Woods with the rest of the brigade. Shortly after reaching the woods, Tilton had his brigade pull back once again due to the retreat of Bigelow's battery. They exited Trostle's Woods, heading northeast across an open field, and took up a position on Cemetery Ridge.[26]

The 1st Michigan experienced a situation similar to that of the 22nd Massachusetts. Colonel Ira C. Abbott had provided protection for his men during Anderson's first assault by having them lie down on the ground while the Georgians' volleys passed over them. Ultimately Abbott ordered his men to return fire, which helped repulse the 9th Georgia's attack. When the Confederates resumed their attack, Abbott was wounded in the face and went to the rear for medical attention. Command of the regiment devolved to Lieutenant Colonel William A. Throop. Throop led his men to the relative safety of Trostle's Woods.[27]

The withdrawal of Tilton had an adverse effect upon Sweitzer's small brigade. General Barnes ordered Sweitzer "to fall back in good order, and to take up a new position a short distance in his rear."[28] Colonel Sweitzer, obeying the order, informed Colonel George L. Prescott, 32nd Massachusetts, of the need to pull back. Prescott, in the thick of the fighting, did not want to leave the position, responding, "I don't want to retire. I am not ready to retire. I can hold this place."[29] Nevertheless, Prescott did retreat, after Tilton's brigade had fallen back. Sweitzer's regiments all complied with General Barnes's directions and re-formed in Trostle's Woods along the northern side of the Wheatfield Road.[30]

The position held on Stony Hill by Sweitzer's brigade was not conducive to a good defense in the event of an attack from the west by the South Carolinians. Only the 32nd Massachusetts fronted the enemy, since Anderson's men were attacking from the southwest through Rose's Woods. The 4th Michigan was reduced to a waiting game, which proved to be deadly for some of the men. James Houghton wrote in his journal that the comrade to his left had "His blouse sleeve torn from his wrist to his elbow throwing the reffuse [sic] of his sleave [sic] in my face."[31] While the Michigan men waited to open fire, many wounded soldiers from de Trobriand's brigade came through their lines.[32]

The 62nd Pennsylvania also experienced difficulties because of its position on Stony Hill. Placed immediately behind the 32nd Massachusetts and in support of the Bay Staters, the Pennsylvanians had the same field of fire problem as the Michiganders—they could not fire cleanly to the southwest. When the second Confederate attack began, the incoming fire at the Federals posted on Stony Hill was severe. Major William G. Lowry was killed during this action. After Tilton's brigade retreated from the hill, Sweitzer's brigade followed suit. In doing so, the 62nd Pennsylvania men moved by the left flank and headed east over Stony Hill until they reached the Wheatfield. There they headed north along the edge of the woods and field, and several men were struck by stray shots. After crossing Wheatfield Road, Sweitzer's three regiments took up a position parallel to the road in the southern portion of Trostle's Woods. The 4th Michigan was on the right (nearest the Peach Orchard), the 62nd Pennsylvania in the center, and the 32nd Massachusetts on the left. Stray shots continued to take their toll on the 62nd Pennsylvania, as Lieutenant Scott McDowell was killed, and several others wounded at that position. The Pennsylvanians were ordered to lie down, avoiding further casualties.[33]

Kershaw's Brigade was the reason for the withdrawal of the two V Corps brigades. He was present with his right wing regiments (3rd and 7th South Carolina) as they reached Stony Hill and pressed the attack, forcing Tilton and Sweitzer to retreat. With Anderson's pressure being applied to Union troops in the Wheatfield to his right, Kershaw's men were in unchallenged control of the hill. He had his two regiments face north to assist in the firing on Captain John Bigelow's 9th Massachusetts battery, which had renewed its raking fire upon Kershaw's left flank. Bigelow's infantry supports had been removed, and he was trying to get his guns off the field to safety. He remembered the retreat from his first position along the Wheatfield Road:

> ...prolonges were fixed and we withdrew—the left section keeping Kershaw's skirmishers back with canister, and the other two sections bowling solid shot towards Barksdale's men. We moved slowly the recoil of the guns retiring them, while the prolonges enabled us to keep the alignment; but the loss in men and horses was severe.[34]

The decision by Barnes to pull his two brigades off Stony Hill must come under question. He had been ordered there to shore up a weak point in Sickles's line. Even though his force was small, he nonetheless had the advantage of placing his men on high ground in terrain that was favorable for the defensive. By allowing Sweitzer's regiments to take up a defense in depth he permitted two regiments (62nd Pennsylvania and 4th Michigan) to be taken off the immediate firing line. He also misread the flow of the Confederate attack, not taking into consideration an attack from the west from Kershaw's Brigade, and instead focusing on Anderson's regiments south of Stony Hill. Once the South Carolinians began their assault across the fields just south of the Peach Orchard, Barnes succumbed to the safety of withdrawal, as opposed to changing front to meet the new threat. Such a movement surely could have been carried out with the 62nd Pennsylvania and 4th

Michigan posted along the top of Stony Hill. Such a realign-
ment may not have stopped Kershaw's attack entirely, but it
would certainly have blunted it for a time, enabling much-
needed Federal reenforcements to reach the scene. Colonel de
Trobriand was not happy about Barnes's retreat, asserting in
his official report that, had the two brigades remained where
they were in support of his right flank, he would have attempted a countercharge against the enemy. Obviously, that
was not to be once Barnes's men withdrew, and de Trobriand
was left to his own devices to extricate his men from a rapidly
deteriorating condition.[35]

The only remaining Federals on Stony Hill were the 5th
Michigan and the 110th Pennsylvania, which were both located on the southeastern slope of the hill. Colonel de Trobriand
positioned himself with the Michigan men, who had lost more
than half of their number. As the Frenchman arrived near the
colors, the colorbearer immediately staggered back, claiming
to have been wounded in the throat. The brigade commander,
while still astride his horse, calmed the worried fellow, who
soon enough realized the bullet had merely glanced off his
leather collar and had not drawn blood. The relieved man went
back to his flag. While this scene played out, Colonel John
Pulford of the 5th Michigan rushed to de Trobriand's side.
Pulford held a revolver in his hand while the two men talked.
Soon the pistol was broken by a stray shot, which struck the
gun but did not harm the colonel.[36]

Increasing sounds of musketry fire on the eastern portion of the Wheatfield alarmed de Trobriand. He sent his acting assistant inspector general, Captain Israel C. Smith, to
check it out. As Smith rode off, a ball tore through the shoulder of his horse, and penetrated his leg. After being instructed
to seek medical attention, Smith cooly saluted his commander,
and "expressed to [de Trobriand] the regret he felt in not being able to be of further service to [de Trobriand], and went off
without hurrying."[37]

With their position in danger of being overrun by Kershaw's and Anderson's men, and with ammunition running dangerously low, the 5th Michigan and the 110th Pennsylvania began to retreat along the crest of Stony Hill. The 17th Maine, faced with similar predicaments, also retreated toward the Wheatfield Road. The men from Maine had endured hard fighting for more than an hour. Sergeant Franklin I. Whitmore of Company D was one of the fortunate soldiers that day. As he recounted in a letter to his parents three days later,

> As I lay in the field near the wall I had no protection but loaded and fired laying down. As I lay upon my back loading a bullet hit me a crack on my head tearing my cap but doing no further injury then to make by head feel a little sore there.[38]

The 17th Maine soldiers kept up their fire along the stone wall. As the pressure mounted, and under de Trobriand's orders, they retreated toward the high ground in the Wheatfield near Winslow's battery. There they halted, firing the balance of their ammunition and whatever ammunition they could procure from wounded or dead soldiers in the area.[39]

It was a difficult retreat for Lieutenant Colonel Merrill's soldiers. The only support they received falling back through the Wheatfield was from Captain Winslow's battery. Fortunately, that was enough. Winslow recalled, "by using shell and case shot at about one degree elevation, and from 1 to ½ second fuse, I kept the enemy from advancing from the cover of the woods."[40] The devastating artillery fire kept the Georgians at bay for only a short time, but it was enough to cover the withdrawal of the men from Maine. The 8th and 9th Georgia regiments were then able to push forward midway into the Wheatfield, while the 11th and 59th Georgia regiments secured their position along the wall.

The southern end of the Wheatfield was cleared of Union soldiers, and Winslow's battery was exposed to enemy musket fire. Kershaw's men advanced northward along Stony Hill and began peppering the Federal gunners and their horses with a telling fire. Captain Winslow withdrew his guns in succession, beginning with the piece on the left, all the while firing his remaining guns. Finally, the right most gun was limbered, and the battery moved to the rear and passed east of Trostle's Woods, where it regrouped for further action. In Winslow's battery, ten men were wounded, eight were missing, and ten horses were killed or disabled.[41]

When the 17th Maine withdrew from the stone wall toward Trostle's Woods, the soldiers suffered some casualties. One unlucky man from Maine was struck in the heel by a spent bullet, which had a heavy impact on him, but did not pierce his boot. Screaming in pain, he fell to the ground. John Haley quickly helped his friend back to his feet, but the stunned soldier, feeling faint, assumed he was dying. He asked Haley to leave him in the trampled wheat to die, which Haley refused to do. Finally, the man was able to hobble toward safety, using his musket as a crutch.[42]

General Birney and Captain Joseph C. Briscoe, one of his staff members, rode up to the position occupied by the 17th Maine near the crest at the northern end of the Wheatfield. The location is marked today with Winslow's battery monument. The regiment had been there for approximately ten minutes and had been resupplied with some ammunition. Birney, seeing Anderson's Georgians entering the southern end of the Wheatfield and advancing toward the Federal position, ordered the Maine men forward in line with bayonets fixed to meet the enemy. He led the advance on horseback, and halted the men midway into the Wheatfield. They knelt in line and began firing at the Confederates, slowing their charge. The position held by the 17th Maine was not strong, and the men soon incurred casualties. Lieutenant Charles W. Roberts was struck in his right thigh, just above the knee, but luckily Lieutenant Colonel Charles B. Merrill quickly cut one of the straps of his sword belt and tied it tightly around

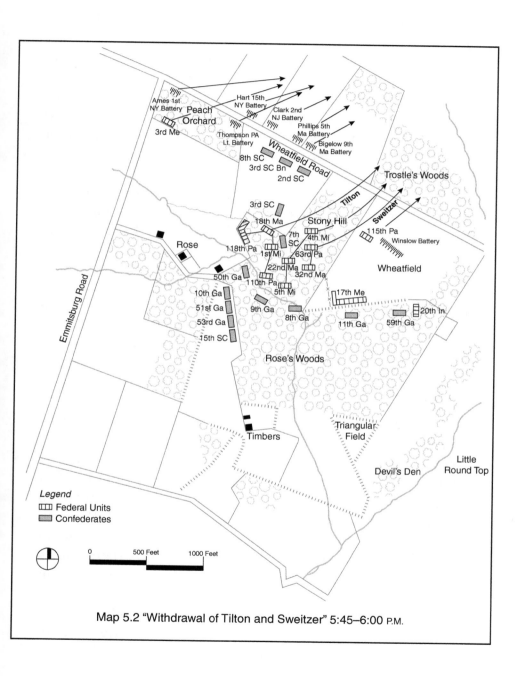

Map 5.2 "Withdrawal of Tilton and Sweitzer" 5:45–6:00 P.M.

Roberts's leg, stanching the flow of blood. The officer then had the lieutenant carried off the field in a rubber blanket. Once he was safely behind the lines, his wound was cared for by an assistant surgeon. Captain George W. Verrill was another casualty of that stand in the Wheatfield. He was also shot in the leg. When he passed to the rear for medical treatment he saw Union supports moving toward the field. This was Brigadier General John C. Caldwell's First Division of Hancock's II Corps. The 17th Maine was finally forced to abandon its position as a result of the pressure in front from Anderson's men, as well as from Kershaw's men atop Stony Hill to their right. Even the presence of the 5th Michigan, which Birney had ordered to take up a position on the right of the 17th Maine, was insufficient to stop the enemy from causing havoc on the Federal position. These Confederates were working their way north along the hill, and effectively poured a flanking fire on the Maine soldiers. The men in the color guard of the 17th Maine were hit particularly hard—only three out of ten escaped uninjured. Corporal Joseph F. Lake brought both colors off the field, and was rewarded by being promoted on the spot to sergeant by Captain Charles P. Mattocks.[43]

Soon the South Carolinians' stronghold on the hill was challenged by the arrival of reinforcements from Caldwell's division. Kershaw saw the approach of the Union soldiers at the north end of the Wheatfield. He refused the right flank of the 7th South Carolina to meet this threat. He also hurried to his right rear to call up his remaining regiment, the 15th South Carolina, which had been assisting Anderson's Georgians in Rose's Woods. Just before Kershaw reached this regiment its colonel, William De Saussure, had been killed leading his men into action.[44]

Kershaw also sought the aid of his fellow brigadier, Paul J. Semmes, whose brigade advanced 150 yards to the right rear of the Gamecocks. Semmes promptly responded and ordered his troops to advance. They moved forward at the double-quick, with the 10th Georgia entering the ravine between Stony Hill and Rose's Woods, approximately one hundred yards to the right of the 7th South Carolina. Once in the ravine, they assisted in slowing the Federal advance. In the meantime, Kershaw hurried back to his men and prepared for renewed fighting.[45]

Paul Semmes pressed forward into the ravine with his men and urged them on. While doing so he was shot in the left thigh, a wound that would prove to be mortal. He applied a tourniquet to himself, with the assistance of a man from the 10th Georgia, and was evacuated to a field hospital. After the battle, Semmes was transported south by ambulance to Martinsburg, Virginia, where he stayed in the house of Mary Oden.[46]

On July 10 Semmes wrote a letter to his wife. Attempting to downplay his injury, he stated that the "main danger [was] over,"[47] and "the wound had done remarkable well."[48] He also told her that his brigade "suffered severely and behaved well."[49] The letter would be his last, for later that day Paul Semmes died with his sword at his side and his Bible in his hand. Mary Oden wrote a moving letter to his widow that same day. In it she touchingly recounted the general's last few days and moments. She informed Mrs. Semmes that her husband was a true Christian to the end. The premonition of death that Semmes expressed in his June 23, 1863, letter had come to fruition.[50]

Semmes's Georgians did not make it into the Wheatfield on their first movement forward. They stalled in the ravine and traded shots with the soldiers of Colonel Patrick Kelly's Second Brigade, known as the Irish Brigade. These Federal regiments (28th Massachusetts, 63rd, 69th, and 88th New York, and the 116th Pennsylvania) were dispatched, along with the rest of Brigadier General John C. Caldwell's First Division of Hancock's II Corps, to shore up the crumbling III Corps line.

John Curtis Caldwell, born on April 17, 1833, in Lowell, Vermont, was one of George Meade's youngest divisional commanders at Gettysburg. Lacking any formal military experience prior to the Civil War, he was principal at Washington Academy in East Machias, Maine, from 1856–1861. Caldwell began his military training as colonel of the 11th Maine in November 1861. A competent commander, Caldwell took control of the First Division, II Corps on May 22, 1863, when Winfield Scott Hancock was promoted to lead the II Corps. Thus, Gettysburg would be Caldwell's first chance at commanding a division in battle.[51]

Caldwell's division had been posted along Cemetery Ridge in the fields just west of the Jacob Hummelbaugh farmstead, approximately three quarters of a mile north of the Wheatfield. Around 5:00 P.M. Lieutenant William P. Wilson, of Caldwell's staff, rode to Colonel Edward E. Cross, commanding the First Brigade, with orders to move south toward the fighting. Cross immediately mounted his horse, issued orders, and led his men into action. Soon his brigade was followed by the other brigades in the division—Kelly's, Zook's, and Brooke's. Passing through Trostle's Woods, Cross was confronted by two aides, one of whom was mounted on a young horse that plunged furiously whenever shot or shell landed nearby. That aide informed Cross that the enemy was moving quickly through the field and would soon break the Federal line. The colonel responded promptly, ordering his men "by the right flank march."[52] This caused considerable confusion, for it served to have the rear rank facing in battle line, with the file closers pushing through. Nevertheless, the desired effect was realized, as Cross's men swiftly crossed the Wheatfield Road into the fighting.[53]

The men of the second brigade in line, the Irish Brigade, had earlier received a battlefield absolution for their sins. Father William Corby, Catholic chaplain for the 88th New York, had received permission from Colonel Patrick Kelly to assemble the men. When they hurriedly came together, Father Corby climbed upon a large rock with his purple stole around his neck. "My dear Christian friends! In consideration of the want of time for each one to confess his sins in due order

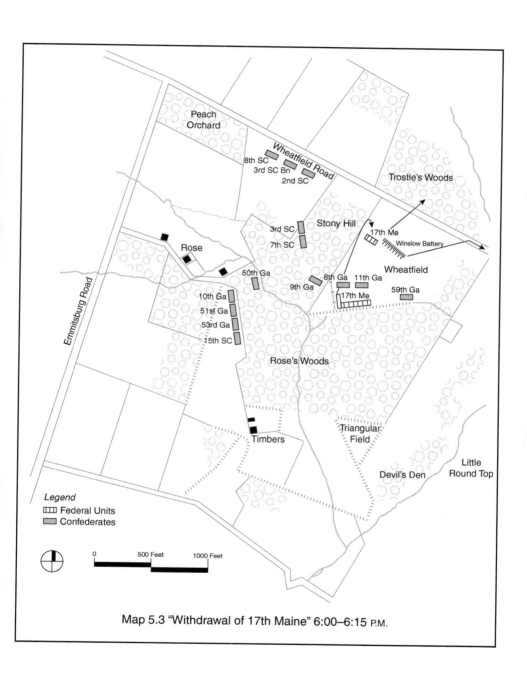

Peach
Orchard

Wheatfield Road

8th SC
3rd SC Bn
2nd SC

Trostle's Woods

3rd SC
7th SC

Stony Hill

17th Me

Winslow Battery

Rose

50th Ga

9th Ga

8th Ga   11th Ga

Wheatfield

17th Me

59th Ga

10th Ga
51st Ga
53rd Ga
15th SC

Emmitsburg Road

Rose's Woods

Timbers

Triangular
Field

Devil's Den

Little
Round Top

Legend

Federal Units
Confederates

0   500 Feet   1000 Feet

Map 5.3 "Withdrawal of 17th Maine" 6:00–6:15 P.M.

as required for the reception of the sacrament of penance, I will give you general absolution...."[54] With that the men, caps in one hand and rifles in the other, knelt and recited an act of contrition. Thus fortified, they swiftly moved south along the ridge, crossed the Trostle farm, and prepared to enter the fray.[55]

Samuel K. Zook's Third Brigade followed Kelly's men. Riding in front of his men, Zook was soon approached by Major Henry Tremain of Sickles's staff. Tremain had been dispatched by a worried Sickles to find reinforcements for his crumbling III Corps position. The major implored Zook to take his brigade and follow him, a serious breach in military protocol, since Zook's superior, Caldwell, had not authorized the movement. Zook, grasping the seriousness of the situation, agreed, and rode off toward the Trostle farm to confer directly with Sickles. When the two generals met, Zook agreed to bring his brigade to Sickles's help. The grateful major general personally directed Zook where the men were to be placed, whereupon Zook immediately rode off to his regiments, jumping stone walls and ditches along the way. Upon reaching his command, he sent staff members to Caldwell to advise the divisional commander of his intention, then led his regiments southwesterly toward the Stony Hill.[56]

The last brigade in Caldwell's division to approach the Wheatfield action was the Fourth Brigade, commanded by Colonel John R. Brooke. Caldwell directed Brooke to move his regiments south, following the Irish Brigade. As Brooke's men neared Trostle's Woods, Caldwell met Brooke in the open fields and commanded him to halt his line. Due to the unusual manner in which the march had been conducted, Brooke's regiments, like those of the other three brigades in the division, were out of alignment as they prepared to meet their foe. When the orders came to move into the Wheatfield, Brooke's men "advanced in line, faced by the rear rank (which formation was necessary, from the fact that there was not time to form by the front rank)."[57]

The first brigade of Caldwell's division to enter the Wheatfield belonged to Colonel Edward E. Cross. It came in on the northeast portion of the field, aligned, from left to right, as follows: 5th New Hampshire, 148th Pennsylvania, 61st New York, and 81st Pennsylvania. The brigade advanced quickly and its front soon extended from the woods on the left (where the 20th Indiana had fought the 3rd Arkansas and 59th Georgia) to the middle of the Wheatfield along the crest of Houck's Ridge. As soon as Union soldiers appeared in the open, some of Anderson's men, posted in the Wheatfield as skirmishers, began a deadly fire. Second Lieutenant Charles A. Hale of the 5th New Hampshire remembered, "the bullets from the enemy's skirmishers came buzzing around like bees, and we could see the puffs of smoke from their rifles in every direction, showing that we were about to encounter a heavy force." The brigade continued to advance quickly, capturing twenty Georgians in the process. One Confederate prisoner was an officer who held nothing but contempt for the Federals. Rather than surrender his sword, he broke it in half at the hilt and flung it at the ground in front of his captor.[58]

Edward E. Cross was the hard-fighting commander of the First Brigade. Born in Lancaster, New Hampshire, on April 21, 1831, Cross lived a full life during his thirty-three years on earth. At age twenty he left his home state for adventure out West. He moved to Cincinnati, Ohio, becoming an editor of the *Cincinnati Times*. During his early years associated with that newspaper he traveled extensively throughout the West and Southwest, filing popular reports with the paper under the name of Richard Everett. His travels fueled a desire for a more exciting life, and he became associated with the Santa Rita Mining Company of Arizona. He also worked as a trapper, hunter, and Indian fighter, successfully fighting one duel with rifles and another with swords. His travels took him into Mexico, where he served for a time as an officer in that country's liberal party army. When the Civil War erupted, Cross returned to his native state and offered his service, receiving a commission as colonel of the 5th New Hampshire. "As an officer, he was a strict and unswerving disciplinarian, punishing with severity any shirking or neglect of duty....Brave to the utmost limit, his command was always in the front, where it performed prodigies of valor. He never asked his men to go, and they did well if they followed closely where he led."[59]

Colonel Cross had a premonition that he would die at Gettysburg. Earlier in the day General Hancock had mentioned to him that "this day will bring you a star," and the colonel's response was, "no, General, this is my last battle." When he prepared for battle he had Charles A. Hale of his staff tie a new, black silk handkerchief on his head. In battles past, Cross had always worn a red bandanna. Hale's hands were trembling as he carried out his task, realizing the significance of the black cloth. Shortly after his brigade took its position in the Wheatfield, Cross moved to the left of his line, occupied by his old regiment, the 5th New Hampshire. This regiment was in the eastern end of Rose's Woods and was taking flanking fire on its left from the 1st Texas and 15th Georgia regiments. It was also hotly engaged with the right wing of Anderson's Brigade, which was slightly refused from the stone wall in order to fight the 5th New Hampshire. While on the left of his brigade line, Cross's premonition came true. He was mortally wounded in the stomach, and died at midnight. His last words were, "I think the boys will miss me."[60]

With the mortal wounding of Cross, command of the First Brigade devolved to Colonel H. Boyd McKeen of the 81st Pennsylvania, who continued to press the attack. The right regiments of the brigade were taking fire from the 8th and 9th Georgia, posted now behind the stone wall, along with fire from Kershaw's 7th South Carolina.[61]

The 5th New Hampshire and the left flank of the 148th Pennsylvania benefitted from their location in the woods where the 20th Indiana had fought earlier. Unfortunately, the remaining two regiments of the brigade, the 61st New York and the 81st Pennsylvania, were out in the open, unprotected, along

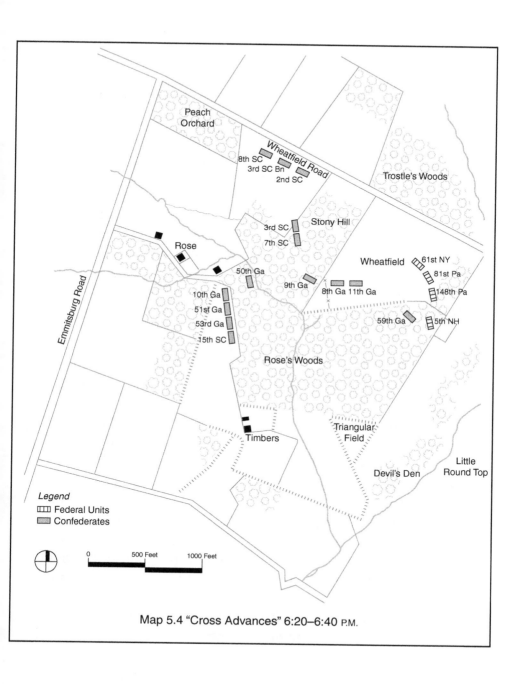

Map 5.4 "Cross Advances" 6:20–6:40 P.M.

the crest of Houck's Ridge jutting into the Wheatfield. Receiving a galling fire from the front and from the right flank, those two regiments began to melt away. Ultimately, Colonel McKeen ordered their removal when reenforcements from the V Corps arrived. However, he kept part of the 148th Pennsylvania and all of the 5th New Hampshire in place for as long as he could. These men ran out of ammunition, yet held their ground until replaced by the U.S. Regulars of Sykes's Corps. One young soldier in the 148th Pennsylvania ran out of ammunition by shooting his rifle at a 45-degree angle into the air, so as to "scare'em"! When they finally pulled back from their position, they received a raking fire from members of Robertson's and Benning's brigades, who had by now taken control of the Devil's Den.[62]

Lieutenant Charles A. Fuller of the 61st New York vividly remembered his time spent in the Wheatfield fighting. His regiment was on the right of the brigade line. Exiting Trostle's Woods the New Yorkers crossed Wheatfield Road, scaled the fence, and entered the Wheatfield. As soon as they reached the crest of the field, the Confederates opened fire upon them. Fuller's comrades fought bravely, save for one second lieutenant who was chastised by Captain Willard Keech for crouching down. Striking the slackard across the back, Keech yelled to the officer to "Stand up like a man!" When the regiment was finally forced to yield the field, Fuller was shot in the left shoulder and in the left leg. Helpless with his broken shoulder and leg, he cried out to two comrades to help him off the field. As they pulled him along, the pain in his arm became unbearable and he had them drop him onto the field. He remained in no man's land, between the two enemy lines, until midnight. At that time Private Phil Confort of Company A in his regiment found him and took him to safety on a stretcher. Fuller was one of the sixty-two casualties suffered by the ninety-member regiment that day.[63]

Brigadier General Samuel K. Zook was born on March 27, 1821, in Chester County, Pennsylvania. He grew up near

Valley Forge and warmly embraced the rich military tradition of the area. An interest in telegraphy ultimately led him to move to New York City, where he became the superintendent of the Washington and New York Telegraph Company. He also participated in the 6th New York Militia, rising to the rank of lieutenant colonel by the outbreak of the Civil War. Zook went with the unit to Annapolis in the summer of 1861, where he served as military governor for the town. On October 19, 1861, he was commissioned colonel of the 5th New York, a regiment he helped recruit. One year later he commanded a brigade, and led his men on the ill-fated attack of Marye's Heights at Fredericksburg. He received the praise of Winfield Hancock for his actions in that battle, and was promoted to brigadier general on March 23, 1863. His brigade participated in the Battle of Chancellorsville, but saw little action. Renowned for his mastery of profanity, Zook was well-liked by his men. However, he, like Cross, had a premonition of his death that day, one which would come true. While his men were streaming into the northern end of Stony Hill he sat astride his horse in the northern end of the Wheatfield near the Wheatfield Road. A shot glanced off a boulder and struck him in the stomach, lodging in his spine. Captain Josiah M. Favill and Lieutenant Charles H. H. Broom of his staff caught their commander as he fell from his horse and led him from the field. He was examined by Charles S. Wood, a surgeon with the 66th New York, who opined that "nothing could be done." Zook was then removed to the G. F. Hoke Tollhouse on the Baltimore Pike, and he died the following afternoon.[64]

The fighting between Zook's men and Kershaw's men on Stony Hill was spirited. Captain Favill was with the 66th New York as it charged. He remembered that they

> rushed at a double quick boldly forward into the mouth of hell, into the jaws of death....we soon came to a standstill and a close encounter, when the firing became terrific and the slaughter frightful. We were enveloped in smoke and

fire....Our men fired promiscuously, steadily pressing forward, but the fight was so mixed, rebel and union lines so
close together, and in some places intermingled, that a clear
idea of what was going on was not readily obtainable.[65]

Jacob H. Cole of the 57th New York was wounded as his
regiment poured into the Wheatfield. A bullet tore through
his right arm, and as his arm went numb a comrade told him
he should go to the rear. Cole simply laughed at the suggestion, exclaiming he was not hurt badly enough to force him
out of the action. Moments later a shell exploded nearby, killing two New Yorkers and shattering Cole's right leg, knock-
ing him unconscious. When he came to, he was surrounded by
Confederates, with one Rebel officer standing on the wounded
leg. Pleading with him to get off the leg, Cole was stunned by
the response. The Southerner drew his sword and said, "You
d— Yankee, I will cut your heart out."[66] Just then a bullet
struck the man in the throat, killing him instantly. When darkness covered the field, Cole made it safely to Federal lines.

When Zook's brigade moved through Trostle's Woods toward the Wheatfield, they encountered members of Barnes's
disorganized troops who had retreated from Stony Hill. There
remains some controversy over the nature of the encounter.
Captain George Meade's account has Zook approaching and
yelling for the men of the V Corps to clear the way. "Barnes
ordered his men to lie down and the chivalric Zook and his
splendid brigade, under the personal direction of General
Birney, did march over them and right into the breach."[67] Major
Thomas Blackburn Rodgers of the 140th Pennsylvania also
remembered having to step over comrades in arms. "A line of
the Fifth Corps was lying down and, as we passed over them,
the boys picked their way gingerly. They called out, 'Don't mind
us; step anywhere; step on us.' They enjoyed seeing us get
between them and the enemy."[68] Rather than attribute any
stigma to this encounter, Harry Pfanz indicated that it was
not uncommon for troops passing to the front in that fashion,

for it was done in similar fashion on other parts of the field as well. Dr. Pfanz does not feel that Barnes's men lacked courage.[69]

As soon as Zook's regiments entered the Wheatfield they advanced in line of battle, with the 140th Pennsylvania on the extreme right. Firing their weapons as they moved forward, the Pennsylvanians reached the crest of Stony Hill. The 140th Pennsylvania had difficulty maintaining its alignment among the boulder-strewn Stony Hill. Nevertheless the men engaged elements of Kershaw's left wing and the 3rd South Carolina in hard fighting. Colonel Richard Roberts of the 140th attempted to untangle his line by ordering a movement to the right. This "cleared our front and carried the right of the Regiment out into the open at the edge of the woods. With ringing cheers we gained this position and immediately come into close quarters with the enemy." Roberts led his right company, Company C, to the right, and shortly thereafter he was killed.[70]

The right of the 140th Pennsylvania Regiment rested near where its present-day regimental monument stands. The center of the regiment extended toward the field sixty to seventy feet southwesterly. The men fought tenaciously, with many taking whatever shelter they could amongst the boulders. Sergeant Ben Powelson of Company K remembered being behind such a boulder and firing seventeen shots into "a bit of timber dark with smoke....The air was hot and heavy with smoke and alive with death or his angels—screaming shells and hissing bullets....Here and there all along the line men were dropping and limping to the rear."[71]

The 3rd South Carolina and the rest of Kershaw's left wing were holding their own against Zook's brigade. The fighting was fierce, with the combatants a mere thirty yards apart. Lieutenant Colonel Gaillard of the 2nd South Carolina remembered the fighting in a letter to his sister-in-law: "The enemy's infantry came up and stood within thirty steps of each other. They loaded and fired deliberately. I never saw more stubbornness. It was so desperate I took two shots with my pistol at men scarcely thirty steps from me."[72]

As Kershaw returned to Stony Hill from his support-seeking mission with Semmes, he became concerned with the advance of the Irish Brigade. Colonel Kelly had swept into the Wheatfield just east of Stony Hill and began advancing on the Carolinians. The brigade attacked in a single line with (from left to right) the 88th New York, 69th New York, 63rd New York, 28th Massachusetts, and the 116th Pennsylvania.[73]

Patrick Kelly was born in Ireland and worked as a farmer in Castlehackett, County Galway, before crossing to America in 1849. When war broke out, Kelly became a captain in the 69th New York Militia, an all-Irish ninety-day unit. He saw action at First Manassas, and when his unit mustered out he became captain of the 16th United States Infantry on October 26, 1861. That regiment was sent to the West, and Kelly led his company in the Battle of Shiloh, April 6–7, 1862. Later that spring he returned east and was commissioned as lieutenant colonel of the 88th New York, a regiment in the colorful Irish Brigade. Promotion to colonel came on October 20, 1862, and when the brigade commander, Thomas F. Meagher, resigned after Fredericksburg in December 1862, Patrick Kelly was given command of the Irish units. He led the brigade until he was killed in action on June 16, 1864, at Petersburg.[74]

Kelly's advance was carried out in dress parade fashion. Lieutenant Colonel Elbert Bland of the 7th South Carolina had been wounded in the thigh but refused to leave the field. Seeing the Irish Brigade proceeding into the Wheatfield, Bland remarked to Colonel D. Wyatt Aiken, "Is that not a magnificent sight?" Aiken remembered that Bland was "pointing to the line of gayly dressed Union forces [Irish Brigade] in the wheatfield whose almost perfect line was preserved, though enfiladed by our fire from the woods, decimating the front line, whose gaps were promptly filled by each file-closer."[75]

The Irish Brigade had only 530 men available for the fighting. The three New York regiments (63rd, 69th, and 88th New

York) had only enough men in each to fill two companies. They were consolidated into one fighting unit, with Lieutenant Colonel Richard C. Bentley placed in overall command of the six companies. During the ensuing fighting Bentley was hit in the left leg by a shell fragment. The seventy-five men from the 63rd New York were armed with .69 caliber Springfield muskets. Earlier that day each man was issued sixty rounds of buck-and-ball cartridges. As the New Yorkers advanced across the Wheatfield towards the southern end of Stony Hill they received fire from members of the 7th South Carolina, who were shooting from behind the protection of boulders. Lieutenant James J. Smith of the 69th New York reported that after his men "delivered one or two volleys, the enemy were noticed to waiver, and upon the advance of our line (firing) the enemy fell back, contesting the ground doggedly. One charge to the front brought us in a lot of prisoners, who were immediately sent to the rear."[76]

The 7th South Carolina was being overlapped by Kelly's men. Kershaw attempted to rectify the situation by bending back the right flank of that regiment, while hoping for Semmes's Georgians to plug the gap. The 50th Georgia made it to Stony Hill and assisted in the standup fighting along with the 3rd South Carolina. Yet, there still remained a gap of one hundred yards between the right of the 7th South Carolina and Semmes's men in the gorge south of Stony Hill. It was this marshy ground that would prove the undoing of Kershaw's position on Stony Hill. With his line being overlapped on both sides, and with the 7th South Carolina giving way, Kershaw ordered Colonel Aiken to reform the 7th's line at Rose's stone wall. His men had fought for approximately half an hour on Stony Hill against elements of the Federal II and V Corps. Now, with the 7th South Carolina having retreated, and with the position of the 15th South Carolina unknown (they were joined with Anderson's Georgians in Rose's Woods) Kershaw ordered a general retreat back to the Rose buildings.[77]

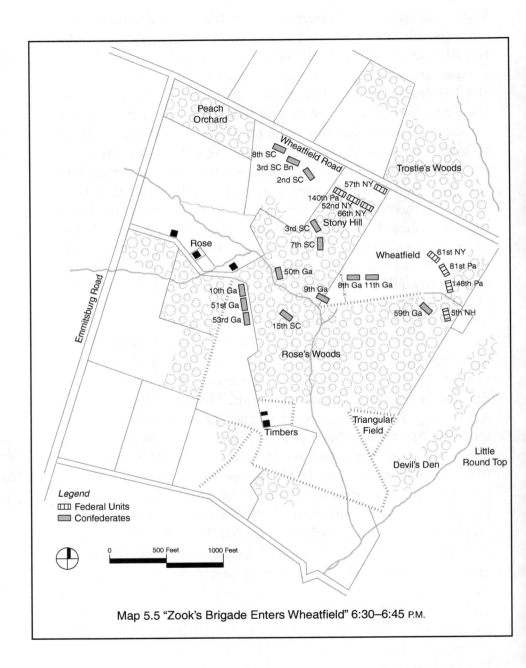

Map 5.5 "Zook's Brigade Enters Wheatfield" 6:30–6:45 P.M.

The South Carolina general followed the lane back to the stone wall located east of Rose's house. The 3rd South Carolina withdrew from the front of Zook's brigade and took position to the left of the 7th South Carolina. They had experienced heavy casualties after the 7th South Carolina had retreated. Major Robert C. Maffett of the 3rd South Carolina believed his men had been fighting for one hour on the Stony Hill. His report indicated that just before Kershaw ordered them back they had come "under a heavy fire of musketry at short range in front, and an enfilading fire of grape and shrapnel from the batteries that the left had failed in entirely silencing, until about dusk, when we were ordered by General Kershaw back to another line a short distance in our rear."[78]

Caldwell's reserve brigade, commanded by Colonel John R. Brooke, was sent into the fight after Zook and Kelly engaged Kershaw. Brooke was born in Montgomery County, Pennsylvania, on July 21, 1838. When the war began he was commissioned as a captain in the 4th Pennsylvania, a ninety-day unit that refused to fight in the First Battle of Manassas. The ambitious Brooke, disheartened with his comrades' actions, raised a new regiment and was commissioned colonel of the 53rd Pennsylvania on November 7, 1861. In April 1863, he was given command of the newly created II Corps, First Division, Fourth Brigade, but retained the rank of colonel. He would lead the Fourth Brigade as a colonel for more than one year, not receiving promotion to brigadier general until May 12, 1864. Caldwell tried to hasten Brooke's promotion along by commenting in his official report that "Of the merit of Colonel Brooke, commanding Fourth Brigade too much can scarcely be said. His services on this as well as many other fields have fairly earned him promotion." When Brooke died on September 5, 1926, he was survived by only one other Union general—Adelbert Ames.[79]

To inspire his men as they prepared to enter the fray on July 2, Brooke delivered a patriotic speech earlier in the day: "Boys—remember the enemy has invaded our own soil! The

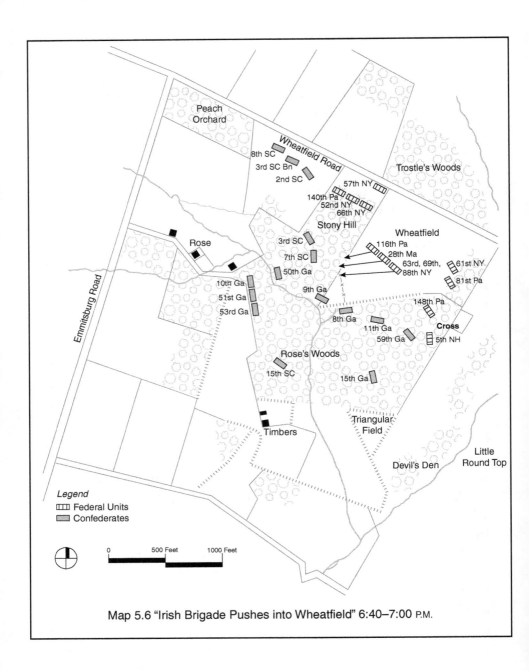

Peach
Orchard

Wheatfield Road

Trostle's Woods

8th SC

3rd SC Bn

2nd SC

57th NY

140th Pa
52nd NY
66th NY

Stony Hill

Wheatfield

Rose

3rd SC

116th Pa
28th Ma
63rd, 69th,
88th NY

61st NY

81st Pa

7th SC

50th Ga

Emmitsburg Road

10th Ga

51st Ga

53rd Ga

9th Ga

8th Ga

148th Pa

11th Ga

59th Ga

Cross

5th NH

Rose's Woods

15th SC

15th Ga

Timbers

Triangular
Field

Devil's Den

Little
Round Top

Legend

⬜ Federal Units

⬜ Confederates

0   500 Feet   1000 Feet

Map 5.6 "Irish Brigade Pushes into Wheatfield" 6:40–7:00 P.M.

eyes of the whole world is upon us! And we are expected to stand up bravely to our duty!" The brigade's ranks had been depleted to the point where it contained only about 850 men at Gettysburg. Nevertheless, when the call to action came, the men pressed forward enthusiastically, seeking to fulfill their commander's wishes.[80]

Upon crossing Wheatfield Road, the Union soldiers paused midway in the field and exchanged shots with the enemy for about five minutes. The regiments were aligned from left to right as follows: 2nd Delaware, 64th New York, 53rd Pennsylvania, 27th Connecticut, and 145th Pennsylvania. Brooke ordered his men to resume their charge, and they did so at the double-quick in the face of a sharp fire from the enemy. As the Federals charged toward the stone wall at the southern end of the field, Colonel Hiram Loomis Brown of the 145th Pennsylvania was severely wounded, and Captain John William Reynolds took over command of the Pennsylvanians. Lieutenant Colonel Henry C. Merwin of the 27th Connecticut also fell during this action. The Confederates challenging this advance were Anderson's Georgians, who originally fired a volley, then began a fighting withdrawal, heading back through Rose's Woods in the same general direction from which they had entered the area two hours earlier. It was during this retrograde movement that a large number of Anderson's men were captured.[81]

During the charge to the stone wall and beyond, the important role played by a regiment's colors in assisting the attack was demonstrated. When the men of the 64th New York stalled in their movement it was not until the colorbearers pressed forward with the flags that the men charged again. There was a price to pay for this, though, as three colorbearers were wounded and one was killed. At another point when the brigade's charge through Rose's Woods bogged down, Colonel Brooke intervened. Grabbing the colors of his old regiment, the 53rd Pennsylvania, he carried them forward himself. His men immediately pushed ahead, ultimately stopping at the western edge of Rose's Woods. There they fought the Confederates, who had assumed a strong defensive position, one which Brooke referred to as an "almost impregnable position on a rocky crest."[82]

The strong advance of Brooke's brigade through the Wheatfield removed Anderson's Confederate presence from the stone wall area. As the Union regiments rushed into the ravine, there were two Confederate regiments posted south of the Wheatfield, along Houck's Ridge, that observed the charge. The 1st Texas of Robertson's Brigade and the 15th Georgia of Benning's Brigade had joined forces in driving remnants of Ward's brigade from the ridge. Lieutenant Colonel Phillip A. Work ordered his Texans to put an enfilading fire into Brooke's men. Colonel Dudley M. DuBose initially ordered his Georgians to pull back behind the stonewall in the triangular field near Devil's Den due to Brooke's movement. However, having done so, his men then joined the 1st Texas in the enfilading fire.[83]

Brooke's advance had outrun his support on both his flanks. He now found himself positioned on the western edge of Rose's Woods, facing the open fields in his front and the Rose farm buildings to his right. His brigade faced Anderson's men on the left, Semmes's men in the center, and Kershaw's men on the right. The Federals had climbed the rocky summit with great difficulty, and now faced a precarious position. The ravine was behind them and the enemy was in their front. A member of the 27th Connecticut, whose regiment was trading shots with Semmes's Georgians, recalled:

> as they appeared upon the crest of the hill, the enemy, drawn up in readiness just beyond, within pistol-range, opened upon them a withering fire. The contest at this point continued for some time. Planting the colors upon the top, the men loaded their pieces under shelter of the brow of the hill, then, rising up, delivered their fire.[84]

L. L. Cochran of the 10th Georgia was in the thick of the fighting at this part of the battlefield (south of the Rose buildings in the field at the edge of the ravine). One of his nearby comrades, Gus Morrow, was shot through the shoulder. Stunned for three or four seconds, Morrow fell dead at Cochran's feet. Lieutenant J. Thomas Key was shot through the neck. Another comrade, George Wilkinson, was shot in the left knee, and as the bullet struck the bone Cochran remembered the sound being like a sharp whip crack.[85]

Private John Jackson Griffin of the 50th Georgia suffered the same fate as did George Wilkinson. A musket ball struck him just above the left knee, shattering his left femur. Griffin, whose wife had died two years earlier on the same date, was taken from the field and his leg was amputated above the knee. When Lee retreated to Virginia, he was one of the many wounded left behind in enemy hands.[86]

The terrain features on this part of the field near the western edge of Rose's Woods caused problems for Brooke's men. The colorbearers in the 27th Connecticut planted their flags at the crest of the hill before them. There the flags were peppered by Confederate bullets, a fate also reserved for any Union soldier who sought to advance over the crest. The men used the protection of the crest to load their guns in safety below the brow, then rose up quickly to fire at the enemy. In that fashion they were able to hold their own, but were unsuccessful in any attempt to further drive the Confederates in their front.[87]

The action during this phase of the fighting did not last long—probably around twenty minutes. There were several reasons for this. First and foremost, Brooke had no support on his flanks. The remnants of Cross's brigade (5th New Hampshire and seven companies of the 148th Pennsylvania) remained behind on the opposite side of the ravine, where they exchanged shots with the 1st Texas and 15th Georgia, both posted near Devil's Den. This enabled Anderson's Georgians to keep up a steady pressure on the 2nd Delaware and 64th New York. There was also a gap on the right of Brooke's line. When he had pushed his men through Rose's Woods, Brooke

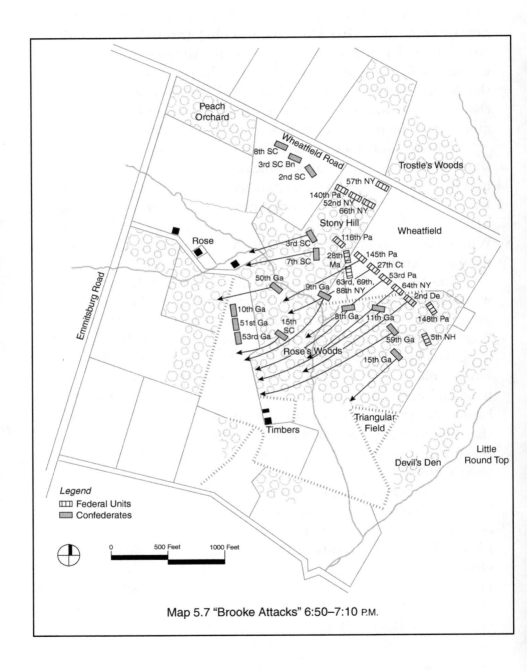

Map 5.7 "Brooke Attacks" 6:50–7:10 P.M.

Peach Orchard

Wheatfield Road

Trostle's Woods

8th SC

3rd SC Bn

2nd SC

57th NY

140th Pa
52nd NY
66th NY

Stony Hill

Wheatfield

Rose

116th Pa

3rd SC

28th Ma

145th Pa

7th SC

27th Ct

50th Ga

53rd Pa

9th Ga

63rd, 69th,
88th NY

64th NY

2nd De

10th Ga

8th Ga

11th Ga

148th Pa

51st Ga

15th
SC

53rd Ga

59th Ga

5th NH

Rose's Woods

15th Ga

Timbers

Triangular
Field

Devil's Den

Little
Round Top

Emmitsburg Road

Legend
▭ Federal Units
▭ Confederates

0   500 Feet   1000 Feet

realized that Zook's and Kelly's men were stalled out on Stony Hill. Certainly they had fought hard there, but when Kershaw withdrew to the stone wall east of Rose's buildings the Federals from those two brigades remained on Stony Hill and advanced no farther. That allowed the men of the 7th South Carolina to enfilade Brooke's men. Another reason for concern was a lack of ammunition, as the Federals only had an average of five rounds per man left.[88]

Brooke reacted quickly. He sent several messages to Caldwell for reinforcements and ammunition. To combat a Confederate (Anderson) presence on his left he refused the left portion of the 2nd Delaware. That regiment's colonel, William P. Bailey, reported that his men were holding out, but without support on their left, they were in danger of being outflanked. Facing that prospect, dangerously low on ammunition, and perceiving a threat from the direction of the Peach Orchard to his right front, Brooke ordered a retreat. Shortly after giving that order, he was wounded in the ankle and left the field with the assistance of two men.[89]

Chapter Six

Wofford Sweeps the Wheatfield

The threat from the Peach Orchard was the advance of William T. Wofford's Brigade, which was following up on the success of Barksdale's Mississippians. Barksdale had been anxious to get into the action; when finally permitted to do so, the brigadier stormed into the Federals along the Emmitsburg Road and the Peach Orchard. McLaws's aide-de-camp, Captain G. B. Lamar, relayed the order to Barksdale. He watched in wonder as Barksdale led his men into battle, with the Georgians clearing everything in their advance, including a picket fence.[1]

Barksdale's charge silenced the enemy's artillery along the Wheatfield Road, and relieved some of the pressure on Kershaw's left flank. When three of Barksdale's regiments (13th, 17th, and 18th Mississippi) wheeled north and began rolling up Humphreys's left flank, Wofford decided to push to the right of the Mississippians. He guided his brigade on the Wheatfield Road and headed east toward the Wheatfield.

Wofford's was the last of McLaws's brigades to go into action. Private John Alexander Barry of Phillips's Legion estimated their attack began around 6:00 P.M. Due to the time frames for the battle action leading up to that point, the attack began closer to 7 P.M. Wofford ordered his men forward at the double-quick. One regiment, the 24th Georgia, had difficulty in passing quickly through Alexander's artillery, and it lagged behind for one hundred yards. Wofford rode over to the regiment and urged them on. As he did so Captain William W. Parker, commanding a Virginia battery, shouted out, "Hurrah for you of the bald-head!" The rest of the artillerymen enthusiastically took up the cheer as the Georgians hurried through their ranks.[2] After the battle Parker wrote for the *Richmond Sentinel*, "Oh he was a grand sight, and my heart is full now while I write of it....Long may General Wofford live to lead his men to victory."[3]

The renewed Confederate assault on the Wheatfield position attracted the attention of both sides as Wofford's Brigade pushed toward the Emmitsburg Road. As it did so, Longstreet was riding in front of the Georgians. He checked his horse and waited for the men to pass him, urging them on as they did. The charge across the field attracted Federal artillery. Colonel Goode Bryan of the 16th Georgia recalled in a letter to McLaws that "a shell exploded and killed and wounded 30 men leaving only 7 men and one officer [in a company]."[4]

By the time Wofford hit the Peach Orchard, Kershaw and his Carolinians were retreating from the Stony Hill. Kershaw was relieved to see "Wofford coming in splendid style."[5] One of the officers of the hard-pressed 2nd South Carolina regiment heard the charging Georgians and shouted to his comrades, "That's help for us! Spring up the bluff, boys!"[6] Wofford rode among his men urging them onward and directing their assault. His brigade overran the remaining artillery positions along the Wheatfield Road, much to the gratitude of Kershaw's left wing. The momentum pendulum was once again about to swing in favor of the Confederates as this new phase of the Wheatfield fight began around 7:00 P.M.[7]

Kershaw's left wing joined the right flank of Wofford's Brigade, and together they pressed eastward toward the northern slope of Stony Hill. They drove all Federal soldiers in their front. The first Union troops who felt this assault were Zook's brigade, with the 140th Pennsylvania being the regiment in the first line of fire. Lieutenant Colonel John Fraser, placed

in command of the regiment upon the death of Colonel Roberts, observed Wofford's men "in large numbers and in good
order marching to outflank us on the right."[8] He held his regiment in position for as long as he deemed prudent, and then
ordered a retreat.

Lieutenant William S. Shallenberger recounted the retreat at the twenty-fifth anniversary ceremony of the 140th
Pennsylvania at Gettysburg:

> [Swept] across the wheat-field, in shattered detachments,
> almost surrounded by the exultant foe, the remnant of
> our strong proud regiment [was] seen to fly, in the dusk of
> that eventful day. Where our line [rallied] we dared not
> guess. The wounded in large numbers were soon collected
> at a little farmhouse [John T. Weikert's house at the north-
> ern end of the Valley of Death] skirting the wheat-field,
> and the rebel soldiers passed on.[9]

Shallenberger was shot in the leg during the retreat. Another Pennsylvanian wounded during the retreat was Lieutenant Jackson J. Purman, who also was shot in the leg.
Purman's luck abandoned him that day, for as he fell to the
ground he was shot in the other leg. He spent the evening
lying wounded on the field. Fortunately, he was assisted by
Lieutenant Thomas P. Oliver of the 24th Georgia the following day. Oliver dragged Purman to safety and left him with a
canteen of water.[10]

Purman himself had attempted to do a good deed for a
comrade, John Buckley of Company B, who lay helpless with
wounds in both legs. Purman and Orderly Sergeant J. M. Pipes
carried Buckley to a point of safety between some rocks.
Purman stayed with the fallen private long enough to
straighten out the wounded man's legs and say goodbye. Ironically, it was this delay with a man who would die later that
day that enabled some of Wofford's Georgians to get close
enough to shoot Purman in the legs.[11]

Wofford's rapid advance led to the capture of many Federal soldiers. Major Thomas Blackburn Rodgers, one of the dozens of soldiers in the 140th Pennsylvania who were captured on the retreat from Stony Hill, had been on the left of the regimental line and had difficulty seeing Wofford's advance. As he was led to the Confederate rear under guard, Rodgers turned over his sword to one of Longstreet's staff officers. Later that evening he saw the young officer "exhibit my handsome sword [to Longstreet] with the remark that he had captured it from a Yankee officer. Of course, I remained discreetly silent."[12]

Wofford's orderly and effective advance had come at just the right time. A member of the 57th New York, the support regiment for Zook's brigade on Stony Hill, wrote of the advance:

> We fell back to the stone wall [north of the Wheatfield Road at the edge of Trostle's Woods], then turned and gave the enemy such a volley of lead as, for a time, disordered his advance....It seemed miraculous that any one came out of that wood alive, so terrible was the fire when we entered it.[13]

Lieutenant Colonel Alford B. Chapman led the 57th New York in the Wheatfield fighting. He had moved his men within fifteen to twenty yards of the 140th Pennsylvania on the right of the brigade line. As he was about to change his front forward to protect the right flank, Wofford's men struck hard. He "held [his] men together until the greater part of the front line had broken through, and then moved to the rear in line and in good order."[14]

Zook's men were confused by the onslaught of Wofford's Brigade against the Federal position on the northern portion of Stony Hill. The Union regiments became entwined with one another while attempting to extricate themselves from their rapidly deteriorating position. Major Peter Nelson, commanding the 66th New York, reported that "men from every regiment in the division were intermingled with ours in one confused mess....the enemy had turned our right flank....I gave orders to retire, which movement was executed as well as could be expected under the circumstances."[15]

The suddenness and shock of the renewed attack by Wofford and Kershaw cleared Stony Hill of Union soldiers. The Confederates quickly pressed their advantage and pursued the fleeing enemy into the Wheatfield. Small pockets of Federals offered some resistance, but were ultimately swept aside. Nonetheless, the fighting was fierce; each side gave as well as they received.

One soldier in Phillips's Legion described the pursuit:

> We went into them with our bayonets and clubbed them with our guns. It was here that I went after the flag; and after shooting one man, and clubbing five others, I was in the act of reaching for the flag when a fellow named Smith jumped in ahead of me and grabbed it. I came very near clubbing him, but he put up such a pitiful mouth about having a family of small children that he wanted to see so bad, I let him have it so he could get a furlough.[16]

Another member of Phillips's Legion experienced the same excited, deadly pursuit indicative of the experience of all the men. John Alexander Barry wrote a four-page letter to his father on July 8, 1863, telling him how they had charged the enemy around 6:00 P.M. and had driven them for a mile. Fourteen men from his company were wounded and one was killed. Several of the wounded were left on the field, including one comrade who had been shot in the arm and bayoneted in the side. Barry proudly informed his father that Longstreet and McLaws both seemed pleased with the charge.[17]

With his division locked in mortal combat with the enemy in the Wheatfield, General Caldwell sought support for his men. He rode up to Colonel Sweitzer, who was positioned with his men in the western portion of Trostle's Woods. Caldwell explained that he needed Sweitzer's brigade to reenter the

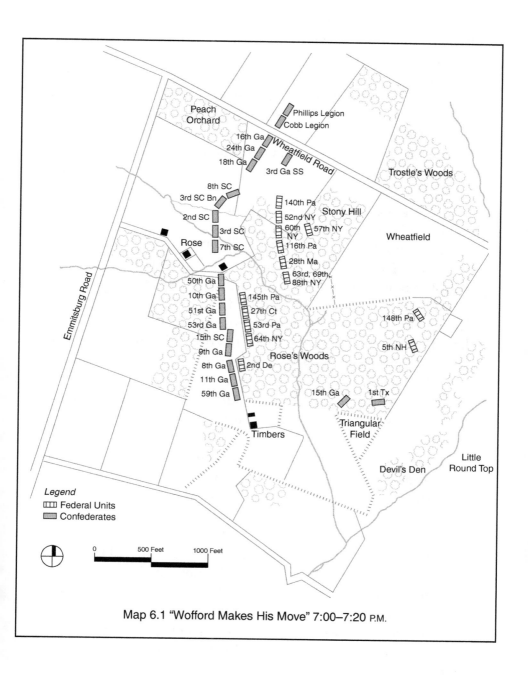

Peach Orchard

Phillips Legion
Cobb Legion

16th Ga
24th Ga
18th Ga

Wheatfield Road

3rd Ga SS

Trostle's Woods

8th SC
3rd SC Bn
2nd SC
3rd SC
Rose
7th SC

140th Pa
52nd NY
60th NY
57th NY
116th Pa

Stony Hill

Wheatfield

28th Ma

63rd, 69th, 88th NY

50th Ga
10th Ga
51st Ga
53rd Ga
15th SC
9th Ga
8th Ga
11th Ga
59th Ga

145th Pa
27th Ct
53rd Pa
64th NY

148th Pa

5th NH

2nd De

Rose's Woods

15th Ga
1st Tx

Triangular Field

Emmitsburg Road

Timbers

Devil's Den

Little Round Top

Legend
⬚⬚⬚ Federal Units
▨ Confederates

0   500 Feet   1000 Feet

Map 6.1 "Wofford Makes His Move" 7:00–7:20 P.M.

Wheatfield fighting, but Sweitzer simply referred him to his division commander, General Barnes, and indicated that he would comply if Barnes gave the order. Barnes was nearby, and Caldwell promptly conferred with him. Barnes acquiesced to Caldwell's request and rode over to Sweitzer to give the order for the brigade to enter the Wheatfield in support of the Second Corps Division. The men were assembled and Barnes made a few patriotic remarks to them, whereupon they immediately charged forward toward the stone wall at the southern end of the Wheatfield. Having secured assistance for his right flank, Caldwell promptly rode to the east seeking General Ayres's support for the left of his division.

Romeyn B. Ayres was born on December 20, 1825, in New York. He graduated from West Point in 1847 along with John Gibbon and A. P. Hill, and his pre-Civil War military career was served primarily in artillery service. At Fredericksburg, the efficient Ayres was chief of artillery for the VI Corps. On April 21, 1863, his fine military record was rewarded, and he was given command of the First Brigade, Second Division, V Corps. The career military man was swept up in the vacuum created by Meade's promotion on June 28, 1863, and Ayres commanded the Second Division, V Corps at Gettysburg.[18]

Ayres acknowledged Caldwell's request and took preliminary steps to move forward through the woods in his front (the same area that the 3rd Arkansas and 59th Georgia had fought in earlier). However, by the time the V Corps soldiers were ready to advance, Caldwell's division was giving way on their right. Ayres recognized this and ordered Colonel Hannibal Day's First Brigade and Colonel Sydney Burbank's Second Brigade to move to the right on the northern extension of Houck's Ridge into the Wheatfield.[19]

Caldwell successfully had Sweitzer's brigade return to the Wheatfield from its position in Trostle's Woods to assist the retreating brigades. Sweitzer's men advanced near the stone wall, with the 4th Michigan on the right, the 62nd Pennsylvania in the center, and the 32nd Massachusetts on the left. Upon taking position, they were fired upon from the right and rear (Kershaw's and Wofford's men on Stony Hill). Ed Martin, Sweitzer's colorbearer, remarked, "Colonel, I'll be d—d if I don't think we are faced the wrong way; the rebs are up there in the woods behind us, on the right."[20] The 4th Michigan was repositioned to face this emergency.[21]

Sweitzer mistakenly believed his right was supported by Federal troops posted on Stony Hill. That was not the case, as elements of the Irish Brigade and Zook's brigade melted across the Wheatfield from the Confederate pressure. Sweitzer ordered the 4th Michigan to change front to face westerly, and followed that order with a command to the 62nd Pennsylvania to do the same. Only the 32nd Massachusetts was left facing south along the stone wall. The colonel dispatched his aide, Lieutenant John Seitz, to explain the precarious position to General Barnes. Seitz rode off, but the divisional commander was nowhere to be found. On his return trip, Seitz's horse was shot out from under him. The lieutenant completed his mission on foot, and ran back to his commander to report his inability to notify Barnes. He also relayed the obvious to Sweitzer—that the brigade was almost surrounded and about to be overrun by Rebels.[22]

As the 62nd Pennsylvania and the 4th Michigan faced west, the 32nd Massachusetts was left to its own devices to stem the enemy tide coming toward the stone wall from the south. One of Sweitzer's staff, perhaps the harried Lieutenant Seitz, approached Colonel Luther Stephenson of the 32nd Massachusetts and ordered him to fall back. Stephenson assumed the order came from Sweitzer, and gave the order for an orderly withdrawal to his men. Sweitzer became furious upon seeing this, and quickly went to the front of the Massachusetts men and demanded to know what they were doing. Stephenson reported that he was only carrying out Sweitzer's orders, whereupon the regiment halted, turned about, and resumed firing at the enemy. The resumed stand was hopeless.

The men in the command were fired at from front, right, and rear. The order to retreat was heard: "Left face, and every man get out of this the best way he can."[23]

The men of Cobb's Legion and Phillips's Legion captured two stands of Federal colors.[24] They were unable to capture the 4th Michigan's flag. Elements of the 18th Georgia regiment of Wofford's Brigade, Kershaw's South Carolinians, and some of Anderson's Georgians, attacked the Michigan men in the Wheatfield. The fighting was hand-to-hand. At some point during the desperate fighting, Thomas Tarsney, 4th Michigan colorbearer, threw down the colors and fled. Colonel Harrison Jeffords saw this and called on Major R. Watson Seage and First Lieutenant Michael J. Vreeland to assist him in recovering the flag. The three men rushed for the flag, and Jeffords grabbed its staff. A wild melee ensued as Rebel soldiers surged around the trio, with the colors being torn to shreds. As the men attempted to fight their way out, Jeffords was bayoneted through the body. The remaining two members of the Michigan trio were also wounded. Seage was shot in the chest and bayoneted in the left leg, while Vreeland was shot twice and clubbed in the head with a musket. Lieutenant Colonel George Lumbard took over command and helped lead the men back across the eastern end of the Wheatfield toward the safety of Little Round Top's northern extension.[25]

The Confederate counterattack drove Zook's brigade and the Irish Brigade from the field. Brooke's advanced position in Rose's Woods was abandoned as Semmes and Anderson applied pressure. During the retreat from the western portion of Rose's Woods, Captain Henry Fuller, Company F of the 64th New York, was wounded. Private George Whipple of the company helped him, but as he did so Fuller was shot in the back and died. Whipple was then captured by a Georgian who demanded that Whipple "Go to the rear you d—d son of a b—h."[26] Brooke considered his retreat as none too soon. "In passing back over the Wheat-field, I found the enemy had nearly closed in my rear, and had the movement not been executed at the time it was, I feel convinced that all would have been lost by death, wounds, or capture."[27]

Brooke's men extricated themselves through the northern corner of the Wheatfield. They retreated through Sweitzer's hard-pressed brigade and passed through two brigades of U.S. Regulars from Brigadier General Romeyn B. Ayres's Second Division of the V Corps. Colonel Sidney Burbank placed his brigade along the Houck Ridge extension, which was occupied earlier by Cross's brigade. Colonel Hannibal Day's First Brigade of Ayres's division was placed behind this line in a supporting role on what is now sometimes known as Day's Hill located in the northwestern end of the Valley of Death.[28]

Hannibal Day seemed born into the military life, for as the son of an army surgeon, he was captured twice with his father in the War of 1812. He graduated from West Point in 1823 and for the next forty years crisscrossed the North American continent, serving in various military posts with the Old Army. On June 28, 1863, he was called from his desk job in Washington to lead the First Brigade, Second Division, V Corps, his first field command in the war. Fortunately for his men, Day was a professional soldier in the true sense of the word, and his cool, calm demeanor served him well in the Wheatfield fighting.[29]

Sidney Burbank was sixty-one years old at Gettysburg. He had been a classmate of Robert E. Lee at West Point, graduating in 1829. By the time the Civil War started, Burbank's health had deteriorated due to his pre-war service around the country with the Old Army. Twice bedridden with hepatitis during 1861–1863, Burbank's first combat action did not occur until the Battle of Chancellorsville. Nevertheless, he was a well-trained, well-disciplined soldier who led his U.S. Regulars admirably at Gettysburg.[30]

After Brooke streamed through Sweitzer's brigade, the 32nd Massachusetts was attacked by Anderson's Georgians, while Kershaw's and Semmes's men drove the 62nd Pennsylvania. Sweitzer's men were nearly surrounded, and he ordered

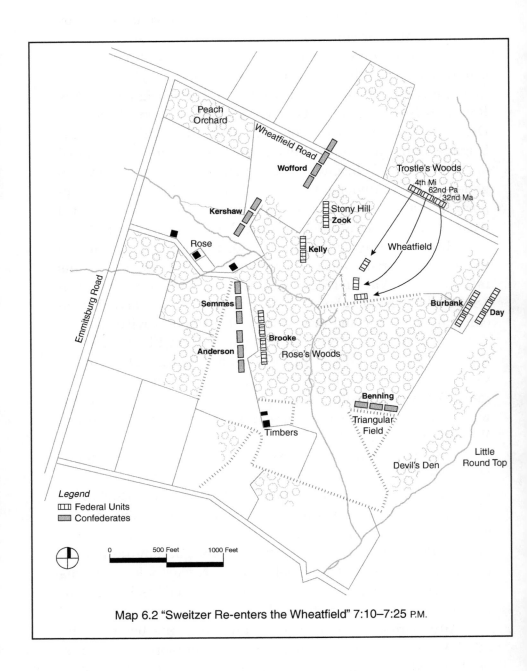

Peach
Orchard

Wheatfield Road

Trostle's Woods

Wofford

4th Mi
62nd Pa
32nd Ma

Kershaw

Stony Hill
Zook

Rose

Kelly

Wheatfield

Emmitsburg Road

Semmes

Burbank

Day

Brooke

Rose's Woods

Anderson

Benning

Timbers

Triangular
Field

Devil's Den

Little
Round Top

Legend
▥ Federal Units
▨ Confederates

0   500 Feet   1000 Feet

Map 6.2 "Sweitzer Re-enters the Wheatfield" 7:10–7:25 P.M.

their retreat. Seeing that the route to Trostle's Woods was cut off by Wofford's men, the Federals retreated diagonally across the Wheatfield.[31]

This maneuver also took Sweitzer's men through the U.S. Regulars' ranks. Burbank's brigade was in place along the eastern portion of the Wheatfield. The 2nd U.S. was on the right, in the open field, with the 7th U.S. to its left. Continuing in a southerly direction along Houck's Ridge toward Devil's Den was the 10th U.S. and the 11th U.S., who were posted behind a stone wall. The 17th U.S. was on the left flank of Burbank's line. Its commander, Lieutenant Colonel J. Surrell Greene, had a difficult position since his men were posted in a gully, with the heights of Devil's Den to their left and rear. Georgians from Benning's Brigade fired into Greene's command, who responded, "the left company of the Seventeenth U.S. Infantry was thrown back to confront this fire and to a more secure position under a slight rise of ground."[32] Day's brigade formed three lines behind Burbank's command. In the first line, the 3rd U.S. was on the right, the 4th U.S. in the center, and the 6th U.S. was on the left. The 14th U.S. was next in line, and the 12th U.S. was last in line. Day's Regulars were on the eastern slope of Houck's Ridge and had precious little protection from enemy fire. Since they were not in position to deliver a concentrated fire to the front (due to being in support of Burbank's brigade), Day ordered his men to lie down. In spite of that precaution the First Brigade still suffered heavy casualties at the hands of Confederate sharpshooters.[33]

Caldwell conferred with Ayres about support for the II Corps First Division; the two generals met near the stone wall along the eastern boundary of the Wheatfield. While they discussed deployment, Lieutenant William H. Powell of Ayres's staff noticed the beginning of the demise of Zook's brigade on Stony Hill. He remarked to Caldwell:

> "General, you had better look out, the line in front is giving way." General Caldwell, who was in conversation with

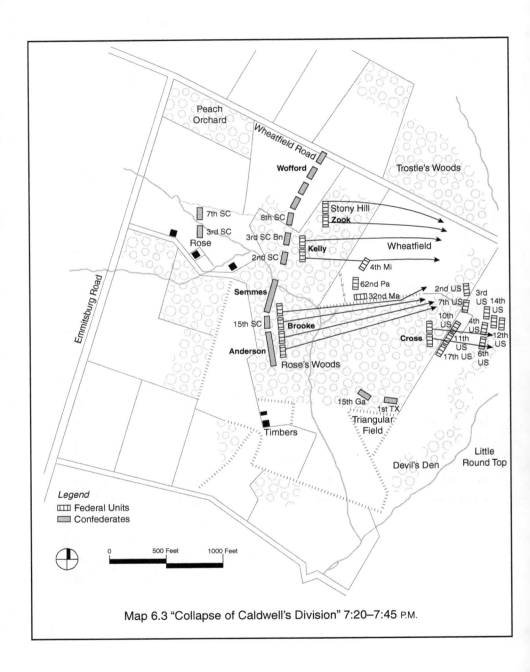

Map 6.3 "Collapse of Caldwell's Division" 7:20–7:45 P.M.

General Ayres, turned and said, in rather a sharp manner, "that's not so, sir; those are my troops being relieved."...In a few moments [Powell] again said: "General Ayres, you will have to look out for your command. I don't care what any one says, those troops in front are running away." At this both generals scanned the battlefield....General Caldwell put spurs to his horse and rode off to the right, along the stone wall.[34]

The rout was now on, and the United States Regulars were called upon to stem the tide.

Major Arthur T. Lee of the 2nd U.S. led his men in a left wheel advance into the Wheatfield. Before they fully completed this movement, the Confederates rapidly outflanked them on the right. Lee ordered his men to halt and commence firing, and the two enemies filled the air with deadly lead. Wofford's Georgians appeared farther to Lee's right, and caused the Federals to retreat. The advance by Wofford's men was so quick and so sudden that Lee believed that "three lines of the enemy, elevated one above the other on the slope to our right"[35] had descended upon him. The terrain does not permit such a formation, nor was the Confederate pursuit carried out in such an orderly fashion at this time. Rather, the Rebels simply pushed forward as quickly and effectively as they could. To a beleaguered regimental commander fighting for his command's safety, it must have looked as perilous as he reported. The firing from the Southerners was so severe that the flagstaff of the 2nd's colors was cut in two, and the colors fell into the hands of the colorbearer. With casualties piling up, and their position being overrun by the enemy, the men of the 2nd U.S. began a fighting withdrawal. They recrossed the eastern stone wall, and headed toward the northern slope of Little Round Top.[36]

The 7th U.S. marched into the Wheatfield with the 2nd U.S. and began a left-wheel movement when the enemy slammed into its right flank. The Federals withstood the initial onslaught and returned the fire. When the order was given to retire slowly, the men did so, but with great reluctance. Their stubbornness was costly though, for by the time they recrossed the eastern stone wall and headed toward Plum Run Valley, they were fired upon from three different directions.[37]

As the right flank melted away, the remaining three regiments of Burbank's brigade faced the Confederate onslaught. The deafening noise of battle contributed to deadly results for the soldiers of the 10th U.S. A large number of the men were unable to hear the command to fall back. When those unfortunate men finally heard the shouted command, they were surrounded on three sides by Longstreet's legions. The 11th U.S. Regulars began their withdrawal from the eastern portion of Rose's Woods. As Captain Thomas Barri led his men across the eastern stone wall, he was dropped by a Rebel bullet. Lieutenants Herbert Kenaston and Henry Rochford, along with four enlisted men, stopped to help their fallen captain. Unfortunately for them a Confederate volley immediately found its mark, and each of the men was hit, with Kenaston dying in a matter of minutes. The 17th U.S., posted on the left flank of the brigade in the low ground, also suffered severely as its soldiers retreated across the marshy ground of Plum Run Valley.[38]

Colonel Day's regiments did not have the opportunity to deploy into battle lines before the Confederate maelstrom rushed through the Wheatfield and struck the U.S. Regulars. Ayres, witnessing the destruction of Burbank's brigade, sent an order to Day to have him retreat back to the northern slope of Little Round Top. Lieutenant John H. Page of the 3rd U.S. was near Day when the colonel received Ayres's order. Day calmly filled his pipe with tobacco and asked Page for a light. As Day bent down toward the match, a bullet tore through the neck of his horse.[39]

The Confederates were now in control of the Wheatfield, Devil's Den, and Houck's Ridge. They were fast pursuing the retreating Federals across Plum Run Valley toward the slope of Little Round Top and its northern extension. The Federals had artillery posted in the area, and hoped that it would stop the onrushing Confederates. Four guns of Battery D, 5th U.S. Artillery were on the crest of Little Round Top. Two guns of Captain Frank C. Gibbs's Battery L, 1st Ohio Artillery were positioned on the northern extension of Little Round Top, while the other four guns were at the base of the hill, commanded by Lieutenant William Walworth. Lieutenant Aaron F. Walcott, commander of the 3rd Battery C, Massachusetts Light Artillery, positioned his six Napoleons along the eastern side of the lane leading from Wheatfield Road north to the John Weikert house.[40]

As the U.S. Regulars came streaming back across the Plum Run Valley, Gibbs's guns provided them with some protection as they fired at the Confederates. "Our front was hardly clear when the irregular yelling line of the enemy put in his appearance, and we received him with double charges of canister....So rapidly were the guns worked that they became too hot to lay the hand on."[41] Not all of the Regulars cleared the artillerists' front before the guns opened up. Lieutenant Page remembered the retreat through that valley of death:

> As we were falling back, we saw the battery officers at the base of Round Top waving their hats for us to hurry up. We realized that they wished to use canister, so took up the double-quick. As I was crossing the swampy ground, Captain Freedlay, 3d U.S., was shot in the leg, fell against me, and knocked me down. When I got the mud out of my eyes, I saw the artillery men waving their hats to lie low. I got behind a boulder with a number of my men when the battery opened with canister.[42]

The U.S. Regulars retreated in an orderly fashion, and turned several times to fire volleys at their tormentors. The Union men refused to break ranks and run even though they were being fired at from both flanks and front. Comrades perched on Little Round Top admired their discipline. One man in Brigadier General Stephen H. Weed's brigade wrote, "for two years the U.S. Regulars taught us how to be soldiers, in the Wheatfield at Gettysburg, they taught us how to die like soldiers."[43]

The valley floor was a living hell for the retreating Regulars. Mud sucked at their boots and slowed their retreat. Then, too, Confederates kept firing at the retreating Federals.

> The few hundred yards to the foot of Little Round Top, already strewn with our disabled comrades, became a very charnel house, and every step was marked by ghostly lines of dead and wounded. Our merciless foes from their vantage ground on our (now) right, poured in volley after volley....Their battalions...poured in a deadly fire on our other flank until gasping and bleeding, we reached Little Round Top and took position behind Hazlett's guns.[44]

The charging Confederates followed the retreating Federals into the Valley of Death. Elements of Brigadier General Henry Benning's Georgians and Anderson's Brigade were on the right of the advance. Semmes's Brigade and Kershaw's 15th South Carolina occupied the center of the line. On the left was Wofford's Brigade assisted by Kershaw's 2nd South Carolina. Kershaw, with the assistance of Lieutenant Colonel Moxley Sorrel of Longstreet's staff, rallied the rest of his brigade and that portion of Semmes's Brigade which did not advance. These men were pushed forward to the stone wall at the eastern portion of the Rose farm. Here they remained in order to check any possible Federal counterattack.[45]

The Federal position on the northern slope of Little Round Top was formidable as the sun began to set. Captain Hillyer of the 9th Georgia recalled the advance against what he referred to as "the strongest natural position I ever saw":[46]

> Our line emerged from the stumpy brush...into a long, narrow but nearly straight opening, which skirted the foot of Little Round Top....I could see to the right and left...thirty-five or forty battle flags, and only from thirty

to fifty men with each. On crossing this opening and going a little way up on the rocky slope...our little attacking column hesitated....I heard no order to retreat and gave none, but everybody, officers and men, seemed to realize that we could not carry the position....By common consent we fell back.[47]

Major Henry D. McDaniel of the 11th Georgia, also of Anderson's Brigade, concurred in Hillyer's assessment of the situation. He reported:

The rout was vigorously pressed to the very foot of the mountain....The loss of the enemy was very great....Nothing but the exhausted condition of the men prevented them from carrying the heights. As it was, with no support of fresh troops...it was found impracticable to follow [the enemy] farther.[48]

The 10th Georgia of Semmes's Brigade also participated in the charge to Little Round Top. Private L. L. Cochran, Company E, was intent on chasing Federals when he came across a wounded Union soldier. The Yankee hailed Cochran, asking his assistance in helping him off some rough stones where he had fallen. Cochran did so and promised to return with water, if possible, after he had finished attacking. By the time the Georgian renewed his pursuit against the enemy across Plum Run Valley, he met his comrades, who were melting back from the strong Union position along Little Round Top and Cemetery Ridge. Cochran fell in with his fellow soldiers, who retraced their steps back near Rose's farm.[49]

Elijah H. Sutton of the 24th Georgia in Wofford's Brigade was captured during the charge across the Valley of Death. His regiment was close to the 16th Georgia as they pressed the attack. Sutton overheard an officer of the 16th urge the Georgians on against a battery (Captain Frank C. Gibbs's 1st Ohio Light, Battery L). Sutton and a few others made the attempt. However, not enough of his comrades were with him, and he was forced to retreat. While retreating he joined in with Patrick

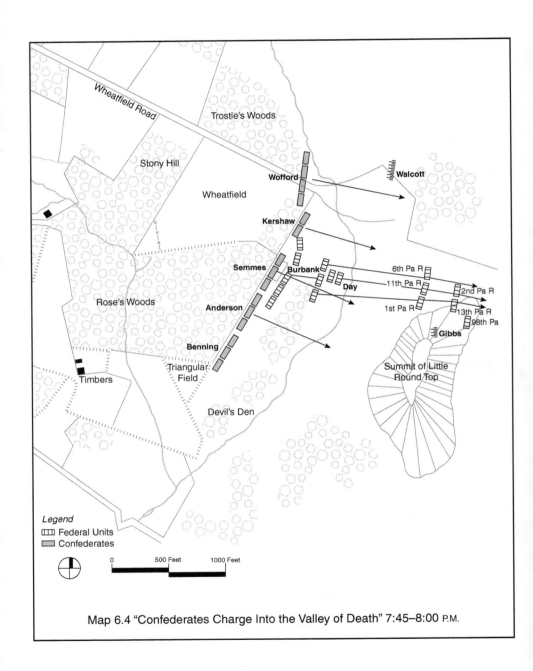

Map 6.4 "Confederates Charge Into the Valley of Death" 7:45–8:00 P.M.

Waddell of his company behind a big shelving rock. Both men were captured when the Federals counterattacked.[50]

Although Wofford's men were unsuccessful in capturing Gibbs's Napoleons, they were responsible for the capture of Walcott's guns. As the Georgians streamed eastward out of Trostle's Woods, the Union battery commander realized his position would shortly be overrun. Having no time to limber the guns and remove them, Walcott ordered them to be spiked. Time permitted only one gun to be so disabled, and all six artillery pieces were abandoned by the Federal gunners as they retreated toward the relative safety of Cemetery Ridge. The captured guns would not stay long in Confederate hands, however, as they would be recaptured shortly by members of Brigadier General Frank Wheaton's VI Corps, Third Division, Third Brigade.[51]

Frank Wheaton was born in Rhode Island in 1833 and entered the U.S. Army in 1855 as a first lieutenant of cavalry. His father-in-law was Samuel Cooper, the top ranking officer in the Confederacy. As lieutenant colonel of the 2nd Rhode Island, Wheaton fought with his regiment at First Manassas and took over as commander when Colonel John Slocum was killed in action. On November 29, 1862, Wheaton was promoted to brigadier general, taking command of the Third Brigade, Third Division, VI Corps. His Third Brigade was commanded by Colonel David J. Nevin, who took over the brigade on the evening before the Wheatfield fighting. Nevin, who had no prior military training before becoming colonel of the 62nd New York, was thus the most inexperienced brigade commander on either side on July 2.[52]

Brigadier General Samuel W. Crawford, commanding the Third Division of the V Corps, organized the Union counterattack against the Confederates in the Valley of Death. Crawford was a physician by trade, and was present in Fort Sumter during its bombardment in April 1861. Colonel William McCandless commanded Crawford's First Brigade. He began the war as a private with the 2nd Pennsylvania Reserves.

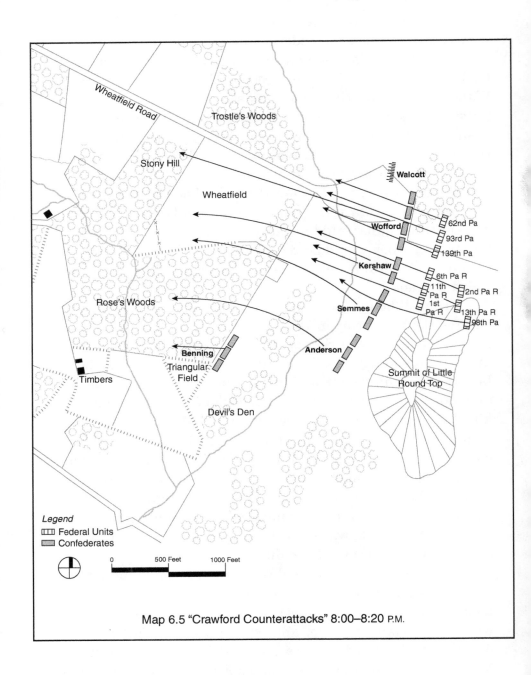

Map 6.5 "Crawford Counterattacks" 8:00–8:20 P.M.

Wheatfield Road

Trostle's Woods

Stony Hill

Wheatfield

Walcott

62nd Pa

93rd Pa

Wofford

139th Pa

Kershaw

6th Pa R

11th Pa R

2nd Pa R

1st Pa R

Semmes

13th Pa R

98th Pa

Rose's Woods

Benning

Anderson

Triangular Field

Summit of Little Round Top

Timbers

Devil's Den

Legend
Federal Units
Confederates

0   500 Feet   1000 Feet

Obviously he possessed outstanding military characteristics, for he was promoted to colonel of the regiment in August 1862. Seriously wounded at Second Manassas, McCandless missed the Battle of Antietam while recovering from his injuries, but led his men at Fredericksburg. On June 25, 1863, McCandless's brigade joined the Army of the Potomac (it had been serving in the Washington defenses since the spring) as it prepared to grapple with the Confederates in Pennsylvania.[53]

Colonel McCandless formed his men into two lines. The front line consisted of the 1st, 11th, and 6th Pennsylvania Reserves. The second line had the 13th Pennsylvania Reserves on the left and the 2nd Pennsylvania Reserves on the right. Slightly to the left and rear of the 13th Pennsylvania Reserves was the 98th Pennsylvania of Brigadier General Frank Wheaton's brigade. The regiment had arrived at Little Round Top minutes ahead of the other regiments in its brigade and became separated from the command. The rest of Wheaton's men arrived at the end of its thirty-four-mile march that day, and filed in north of McCandless's men. The 139th Pennsylvania was on the left, 93rd Pennsylvania in the center, and the 62nd Pennsylvania was on the right.[54]

The double canister blasts from Gibbs's guns had an effect on the exhausted Confederates, and they lost steam in their pursuit of the retreating U.S. Regulars. Nevertheless, as they approached the base of the northern slope of Little Round Top, the Federals posted there waited to test their mettle against the Southerners. Finally, Crawford decided he could wait no longer for retreating Union soldiers to make it to safety behind his lines, for the enemy was close at hand. He gave the order to charge, and the Reserves responded by delivering two volleys against the Confederates, followed promptly by a charge. The men in McCandless's brigade surged down the slope at a run, driving the enemy from their front. Crawford joined in the charge, riding his horse near the front line of his men. When the 1st Pennsylvania Reserves's flag became entangled in a tree or bush, Crawford grabbed the staff from the colorbearer and pulled the flag loose. He then carried the flag down the slope and across Plum Run Valley, with the anxious colorbearer, Corporal Bertless Slott, staying right by his side. The relieved Slott finally had the colors returned to him at the far side of the valley.[55]

No one had ordered a retreat for the men in the brigades of Benning, Anderson, Kershaw, or Semmes, yet when the counterattack came, these exhausted Confederates withdrew. This was not the case for Wofford's Brigade. They had been ordered back by General Longstreet, much to their displeasure. Colonel Goode Bryan of the 16th Georgia, whose regiment had advanced the farthest of Wofford's men, recounted the situation to McLaws after the war:

> I can and do assert, most positively, that they [16th Georgia] were not driven back, and that there was no enemy in front, nor on the right, to cause us to fall back; and I further assert that I was ordered back by a courier sent by the Commanding General Longstreet, and that before going, seeing Gen. Longstreet some distance in the rear, I went to him and requested him not to order us back, but he repeated the order, and I retired.[56]

Bryan never forgave Longstreet for pulling the brigade back. In 1877 he wrote to McLaws, "I have always thought that if Gen L had not ordered us to fall back we could have won the day."[57]

General Wofford was extremely angry over Longstreet's order to withdraw. The brigadier felt his Georgians had driven the enemy from the field and should have been allowed to remain in their advance position. He expressed to McLaws consternation that his withdrawal may be misconstrued. McLaws ordered Wofford to re-form his brigade across the Wheatfield Road near the northern extension of Stony Hill. Their position placed them just west of Trostle's Woods. Longstreet's justification for giving the order to retreat asserted that fresh Union troops were being funneled into the action.[58]

Assisting Crawford's Pennsylvania Reserves in chasing Wofford's men were the men of General Wheaton's brigade. They had been rushed into position along Cemetery Ridge. When the Reserves pressed into the Valley in their counterattack, Wheaton's men soon followed on the right flank in support, heading west on the north side of the Wheatfield Road. Their momentum eventually took them to the eastern end of Trostle's Woods. By then Wofford's Georgians had retreated to the other side of those woods. Since the ground was marshy where they were, Wheaton's men shifted their line one hundred yards east, taking up a position where Walcott's guns were placed along the John Weikert lane.[59]

Two of Anderson's regiments, the 9th and 11th Georgia, made a stand at the stone wall along the crest of Houck's Ridge. This brief, but effective, resistance stemmed the rush of McCandless's Pennsylvanians. Shortly thereafter Anderson's Brigade, as well as the rest of the Confederate brigades of Benning, Kershaw, and Semmes, pulled back across the Wheatfield. Anderson's men took up their previous positions in Rose's Woods, as did Benning's and Semmes's Georgians. The South Carolinians re-formed near Stony Hill, while Wofford's men extended the Confederate line to the north, bending westerly toward the Peach Orchard. Pickets were sent into the southern portion of the Wheatfield, and for approximately one hour after sunset shots were exchanged between the two enemy forces. Then the firing stopped, and the groans of the wounded could be heard all night from the Wheatfield.[60]

Chapter Seven

Aftermath

For over three hours during the late afternoon of July 2, 1863, a violent struggle ensued in the Wheatfield. When it was over, only the dead and wounded remained in the field.

> In every direction among the bodies was the debris of battle-haversacks, canteens of tin and wood, every kind of rifle or musket, blankets, cartridge-boxes, and bayonet-scabbards, all strewed the ground. Caps and hats with the Maltese cross were mixed with the broad sombrero of the Texans; every conceivable part of the equipment of a soldier of the blue or gray mingled with the bodies of Yankee and rebel, friends and foes, perchance father and son....Corpses, strewed the ground at every step. Arms, legs, heads, and parts of dismembered bodies were scattered about, and sticking among the rocks, and against the trunks of trees, hair, brains, and entrails and shreds of human flesh still hung.[1]

Parts of six Confederate brigades entered the Wheatfield fighting on July 2, 1863. The casualties they suffered gave testament to their determination and fighting spirit. Twenty-two Rebel regiments, containing 7,661 men, were engaged in the hotly contested fight for Mr. Rose's field. Of those men, 497 were killed, 1,475 were wounded, and 487 men were missing in action, a staggering 32-percent casualty rate. The

Southerners confronted elements of four different Union corps, containing thirteen brigades comprised of thirty-nine regiments. The Union soldiers enjoyed numerical superiority, as 12,783 Northern soldiers participated in the fighting. Of those, 29.8 percent were casualties, as Meade's men suffered 539 killed, 2,693 wounded, and 444 missing in action, for an aggregate casualty figure of 3,676 men.[2]

The Confederate assault in the Wheatfield lacked an overall unity that might have contributed to greater gains. The initial striking force in the area belonged to Anderson's Brigade of Hood's Division. That brigade went into the fight at a four hundred-man disadvantage. The 7th Georgia had to protect Longstreet's right flank near the Kern house on Emmitsburg Road, a role usually assigned to Stuart's absent cavalrymen. When Anderson met strong resistance, he had to disengage the enemy and seek assistance from Kershaw's men. The Confederate *en echelon* attack did not proceed smoothly or in a timely manner, and Anderson had to wait for the 15th South Carolina to come up. Then, too, the troops to the left of Anderson's men were from McLaws's Division, contributing to the lack of continuity. Hood went down early in the attack and his successor, Brigadier General Evander Law, was on the right wing of Hood's Division, unable to coordinate the assault with McLaws.

It is ultimately the corps commander's responsibility to keep his divisions on target and on time. James Longstreet was certainly present during that afternoon's fighting, and therefore in a position to oversee the Confederate effort. However, it does not appear that he actively controlled his assaulting columns. In fact, his delay in sending Barksdale's Mississippians forward earlier caused havoc on Kershaw's left. Had Barksdale's men hit the Peach Orchard while Kershaw's men fought toward Stony Hill, the Federal artillery posted along the Wheatfield Road would not have raked Kershaw's left wing. Kershaw himself was surprised that Barksdale had not been sent in earlier.

Of the six Southern brigadier generals whose troops fought in the Wheatfield, Joseph Kershaw stands out. He was the only Confederate commander on the field who attempted to coordinate the division's actions. Early in the assault, he conferred with Semmes, and later on he resumed the offensive with Wofford's Brigade. Of course, Semmes's mortal wounding took him out of the action, and the regiments of his brigade fought the balance of the day mostly as separate units with no real brigade-level direction. Wofford and his men got into the fight last and accomplished much in their drive to Cemetery Ridge. However, the lateness of the hour and Longstreet's order to fall back stripped the Georgians of any chance to exploit their earlier successes. George T. Anderson's efforts that day were exemplary for the short time he was on the field. He brought his troops into Rose's Woods and properly deployed them to strike the Union soldiers in the Wheatfield. When the attack began to bog down, he extricated his men from the enemy and sought assistance from Kershaw. Unfortunately for Robert E. Lee, Anderson's wounding shortly thereafter deprived the Confederate chieftain of a capable officer whose talents most certainly would have benefitted the Southern attack had he remained on the field. The Georgians of Anderson's Brigade had performed splendidly. They had fought for more than three hours, being the only brigade on either side to be in the fight from start to finish. They inflicted severe casualties upon the enemy, but their effort was not without sacrifice. Anderson remembered thirteen years after the battle:

> I know we were in a very hot place during the fight as witness the 8th Ga. Regt. When we entered the fight this regt. had 36 officers on duty and at the close only 6 were unhurt. In my brigade of 5 regts. (the 7th Ga not engaged...) the youngest Lt. Col. in the brigade was in command. My military family staff & couriers ten men and out of this number 7 were killed or wounded. I can not now recollect total casualties, but my loss was very heavy.[3]

The four regiments of the brigade that went into the Wheatfield contained 1,497 men. Of these, 47 percent were killed, wounded, captured, or missing in action. The 8th Georgia suffered a 55.1 percent loss (172 out of 312), the 9th Georgia suffered a 55.6 percent loss (189 out of 340), and the 11th Georgia suffered a 64.8 percent loss (201 out of 310). The greater than 50 percent casualty rate in these three regiments place them among the top twenty-five Confederate regiments sustaining a greater than 50 percent loss at Gettysburg. The 11th Georgia (156) and 9th Georgia (123) were among the top twenty Confederate regiments with the greatest number of wounded at Gettysburg.[4]

The other two brigadier generals (Robertson and Benning) whose troops contributed to the Wheatfield action did not actively participate in that fighting. Rather, they concerned themselves, and rightfully so, with coordinating efforts in and around Devil's Den, and thus were not a factor in the overall Confederate action for the Wheatfield.

The fighting in the Wheatfield at Gettysburg on July 2, 1863, was essentially a regiment-versus-regiment fight. The success and failure attained there came about primarily as the result of the actions of the rank and file soldiers on both sides. These men fought under confusing, deadly circumstances. Often one regiment's activities were unknown to an adjoining regiment, as the terrain, smoke, and noise led to rapidly deteriorating combat conditions. That the soldiers battled each other tenaciously for over three hours, stopping only after darkness set in, is a tribute to the common soldier, North and South, who fought out of loyalty to his country and his comrades. Those sentiments were movingly summed up by one of the colorbearers of the 8th South Carolina, who recalled his memories of the flag and his fellow soldiers:

> We never saw our old flag again, but I would like to stand once more under its folds and let memory bring back some of the scenes when this same flag waived over so many victorious fields, while I can but remember that in its shadow I have seen some of my dearest friends yield up their noble lives for their country.[5]

Appendix A

Confederate Troops Fighting in the Wheatfield

Lieutenant General James Longstreet's Corps
Major General John Bell Hood's Division
Brigadier General Jerome B. Robertson's Brigade

Unit	Engaged	Casualties	Killed	Wounded	MIA	% loss
3rd Ark.	479	182	41	101	40	38.0
1st Tex.	426	97	29	46	22	22.8
	905	279	70	147	62	30.8

Brigadier General Henry L. Benning's Brigade

Unit	Engaged	Casualties	Killed	Wounded	MIA	% loss
15th Ga.	368	171	14	58	99	46.5

Brigadier General George T. Anderson's Brigade

Unit	Engaged	Casualties	Killed	Wounded	MIA	% loss
8th Ga.	312	172	35	108	29	55.1
9th Ga.	340	189	34	123	32	55.6
11th Ga.	310	201	40	156	5	64.8
59th Ga.	525	142	37	75	30	27.0
	1,487	704	146	462	96	47.3

Major General Lafayette McLaws's Division
Brigadier General Joseph B. Kershaw's Brigade

Unit	Engaged	Casualties	Killed	Wounded	MIA	% loss
2nd S.C.	412	169	52	100	17	41.0
3rd S.C.	406	87	22	59	6	21.4
7th S.C.	408	110	24	79	7	27.0

8th S.C.	300	100	26	74	0	33.3
15th S.C.	448	137	23	96	18	30.6
3rd S.C. Batt.	203	46	12	31	3	22.7
	2,177	649	159	439	51	29.8

Brigadier General Paul J. Semmes's Brigade

Unit	Engaged	Casualties	Killed	Wounded	MIA	% loss
10th Ga.	303	97	13	73	11	32.0
50th Ga.	302	92	16	62	14	30.5
51st Ga.	303	95	15	40	40	31.4
53rd Ga.	422	97	28	61	8	23.0
	1,330	381	72	236	73	28.6

Brigadier General William T. Wofford's Brigade

Unit	Engaged	Casualties	Killed	Wounded	MIA	% loss
16th Ga.	303	106	14	49	43	35.0
18th Ga.	302	36	3	16	17	11.9
24th Ga.	303	83	8	29	46	27.4
Cobb's Leg.	213	22	5	17	0	10.3
Phillips's Leg.	273	28	6	22	0	10.3
	1,394	275	36	133	106	19.7

Appendix B

Federal Troops Fighting in the Wheatfield

Major General Winfield Scott Hancock's II Corps
Brigadier General John C. Caldwell's First Division
Colonel Edward E. Cross's First Brigade

Unit	Engaged	Casualties	Killed	Wounded	MIA	% loss
5th N.H.	179	80	27	53	0	44.7
61st N.Y.	104	61	5	56	0	58.6
81st Pa.	175	62	5	49	8	35.4
148th Pa.	392	125	19	101	5	31.9
	850	328	56	259	13	38.6

Colonel Patrick Kelly's Second Brigade

Unit	Engaged	Casualties	Killed	Wounded	MIA	% loss
28th Mass.	224	100	8	57	35	44.6
63rd N.Y.	75	23	5	10	8	30.7
69th N.Y.	75	25	5	14	6	33.3
88th N.Y.	90	28	7	17	4	31.1
116th Pa.	66	22	2	11	9	33.3
	530	198	27	109	62	37.4

Brigadier General Samuel K. Zook's Third Brigade

Unit	Engaged	Casualties	Killed	Wounded	MIA	% loss
52nd N.Y.	134	38	2	26	10	28.4
57th N.Y.	175	34	4	28	2	19.4
66th N.Y.	147	44	5	29	10	29.9
140th Pa.	515	241	37	144	60	46.8
	971	357	48	227	82	36.8

Colonel John R. Brooke's Fourth Brigade

Unit	Engaged	Casualties	Killed	Wounded	MIA	% loss
27th Conn.	75	37	10	23	4	49.3
2nd Del.	234	84	11	61	12	35.9
64th N.Y.	204	98	15	64	19	48.0
53rd Pa.	135	80	7	67	6	59.3
145th Pa.	202	90	11	69	10	44.6
	850	389	54	284	51	45.8

Major General Daniel E. Sickles's III Corps
Major General David B. Birney's First Division
Brigadier General J. H. Hobart Ward's Second Brigade

Unit	Engaged	Casualties	Killed	Wounded	MIA	% loss
20th Ind.	401	156	32	114	10	38.9
99th Pa.	277	110	18	81	11	39.7
	678	266	50	195	21	39.2

Colonel P. Regis de Trobriand's Third Brigade

Unit	Engaged	Casualties	Killed	Wounded	MIA	% loss
17th Maine	350	133	18	112	3	38.0
3rd Mich.	237	45	7	31	7	18.9
5th Mich.	216	109	19	86	4	50.5
110th Pa.	152	53	8	45	0	34.9
	955	340	52	274	14	35.6

Brigadier General Andrew A. Humphreys's Second Division
Colonel George C. Burling's Third Brigade

Unit	Engaged	Casualties	Killed	Wounded	MIA	% loss
8th N.J.	170	47	7	38	2	27.6
115th Pa.	151	24	3	18	3	15.9
	321	71	10	56	5	22.1

Captain George E. Randolph's Artillery Brigade
Captain George B. Winslow's 1st New York Light, Battery B

Engaged	Casualties	Killed	Wounded	MIA	% loss
116	18	0	10	8	15.5

Captain A. Judson Clark's New Jersey Light, 2d Battery

Engaged	Casualties	Killed	Wounded	MIA	% loss
131	20	1	16	3	15.3

Major General George Sykes's V Corps
Brigadier General James Barnes's First Division
Colonel William S. Tilton's First Brigade

Unit	Engaged	Casualties	Killed	Wounded	MIA	% loss
18th Mass.	139	27	1	23	3	19.4
22nd Mass.	137	31	3	27	1	22.6
1st Mich.	145	42	5	33	4	29.0
118th Pa.	233	25	3	19	3	10.7
	654	125	12	102	11	19.1

Colonel Jacob B. Sweitzer's Second Brigade

Unit	Engaged	Casualties	Killed	Wounded	MIA	% loss
32nd Mass.	242	80	13	62	5	33.1
4th Mich.	342	165	25	64	76	48.2
62nd Pa.	426	175	28	107	40	41.1
	1,010	420	66	233	121	41.6

Brigadier General Romeyn B. Ayres's Second Division
Colonel Hannibal Day's First Brigade

Unit	Engaged	Casualties	Killed	Wounded	MIA	% loss
3rd U.S.	300	73	6	66	1	24.3
4th U.S.	173	40	10	30	0	23.1
6th U.S.	196	44	4	40	0	22.4
12th U.S.	413	92	8	71	13	22.3
14th U.S.	490	132	18	110	4	26.9
	1,572	381	46	317	18	24.2

Colonel Sidney Burbank's Second Brigade

Unit	Engaged	Casualties	Killed	Wounded	MIA	% loss
2nd U.S.	201	67	6	55	6	33.3
7th U.S.	116	59	12	45	2	50.9
10th U.S.	93	51	16	32	3	54.8
11th U.S.	286	120	19	92	9	42.0
17th U.S.	260	150	25	118	7	57.7
	956	447	78	342	27	46.8

Brigadier General Samuel W. Crawford's Third Division
Colonel William McCandless's First Brigade

Unit	Engaged	Casualties	Killed	Wounded	MIA	% loss
1st Pa. Res.	377	46	8	38	0	12.2
2nd Pa. Res.	232	37	3	33	1	15.9
6th Pa. Res.	323	24	2	22	0	7.4
13th Pa. Res.	297	48	7	39	2	16.2
	1,229	155	20	132	3	12.6

Captain Augustus P. Martin's Artillery Brigade
Captain Frank C. Gibbs's 1st Ohio Light, Battery L

Engaged	Casualties	Killed	Wounded	MIA	% loss
113	2	0	2	0	1.8

Lieutenant Aaron F. Walcott's Massachusetts Light, 3d Battery (C)

Engaged	Casualties	Killed	Wounded	MIA	% loss
115	6	0	6	0	5.2

Major General John Sedgwick's VI Corps
Brigadier General Frank Wheaton's Third Division
Colonel David J. Nevin's Third Brigade

Unit	Engaged	Casualties	Killed	Wounded	MIA	% loss
62nd N.Y.	237	12	1	11	0	5.1
93rd Pa.	234	10	0	10	0	4.3
98th Pa.	351	11	0	11	0	0.3
139th Pa.	443	20	1	19	0	4.5
	1,265	53	2	51	0	4.2

Brigadier General Robert O. Tyler's Artillery Reserve
Lieutenant Colonel Freeman McGilvery's
First Volunteer Brigade
Captain Charles A. Phillips's Massachusetts Light, 5th Battery (E)

Engaged	Casualties	Killed	Wounded	MIA	% loss
104	21	4	17	0	20.2

Captain John Bigelow's Massachusetts Light, 9th Battery

Engaged	Casualties	Killed	Wounded	MIA	% loss
104	28	8	18	2	26.9

Captain Patrick Hart's New York Light, 15th Battery

Engaged	Casualties	Killed	Wounded	MIA	% loss
70	16	3	13	0	22.9

Captain James Thompson's Pennsylvania Light, Batteries C and F

Engaged	Casualties	Killed	Wounded	MIA	% loss
105	28	2	23	3	26.7

Captain Robert H. Fitzhugh's Fourth Volunteer Brigade
Captain Nelson Ames's 1st New York Light, Battery G

Engaged	Casualties	Killed	Wounded	MIA	% loss
84	7	0	7	0	8.3

Notes

Abbreviations

The following abbreviations are used in the notes:

OR   U.S. War Department. *The War of the Rebellion: A Compilation of the Official Records of the Union and Confederate Armies.* 128 vols. Washington, D.C.: U.S. Government Printing Office, 1880–1901.

SHSP Southern Historical Society Papers, Dayton, Ohio: Broadfoot Publishing Company/ Morningside House, 1990.

Chapter One

1. John W. Busey and David G. Martin, *Regimental Strengths and Losses at Gettysburg* (Hightstown, N.J.: Longstreet House, 1986), 312.

2. See appendix A and appendix B for Confederate and Federal units involved in the fighting in the Wheatfield.

3. Eric Campbell, "Caldwell Clears the Wheatfield," *Gettysburg Historical Articles of Lasting Interest* (July 1990), 48.

4. Biographical information on G.T. Anderson: *Confederate Veteran* 9 (1901), 418; Ezra Warner, *Generals in Gray: Lives of the Confederate Commanders* (Baton Rouge: Louisiana State University Press, 1959), 6–7; Richard N. Current, ed., *Encyclopedia of the Confederacy* (New York: Simon & Schuster, 1993) 1:30; Clement A. Evans, *Confederate Military History: Extended Edition* (Wilmington, N.C.: Broadfoot Publishing, 1987) 7:391–92; 8:461–62.

5. Robert K. Krick, *Lee's Colonels: A Biographical Register of the Field Officers of the Army of Northern Virginia*, 4th ed. (Dayton, Ohio: Morningside House, Inc. 1992), 374.

6. Regimental strengths, as reported on June 30, 1863, provided in Busey and Martin, *Regimental Strengths and Losses*, 135; biographical information provided in Krick, *Lee's Colonels*, 152, 217, 240, 244–45, 249, 284, 374, 393.

7. Biographical information on Lafayette McLaws in Association of Graduates, U.S. Military Academy, Annual Reunion, June 9, 1898; Warner, *Generals in Gray*, 204–5; Jack D. Welsch, M.D., *Medical Histories of Confederate Generals* (Kent, Ohio: The Kent State University Press, 1995), 150; Stewart Sifakis, *Who Was Who in the Civil War* (New York and Oxford: Facts on File Publications, 1988), 420; Larry Tagg, *The Generals of Gettysburg* (Mason City, Iowa: Savas Publishing Company, 1998), 209–11.

8. Biographical information on Joseph B. Kershaw in Warner, *Generals in Gray*, 171; Sifakis, *Who Was Who in the Civil War*, 360–61; *Confederate Military History Extended Edition*, 6:409–11.

9. United States War Department, *The War of the Rebellion: A Compilation of the Official Records of the Union and Confederate Armies,* 70 vols. in 128 pts. (Washington: Government Printing Office, 1880–1901), ser. 1, vol. 27, pt. 2, 362 (hereinafter cited as *OR,* followed by appropriate volume and part, all ser. 1 unless noted).

10. Joseph H. Crute, Jr., *Units of the Confederate States Army* (Gaithersburg, Md.: Olde Soldier Books, Inc. 1987), 249–50; Mac Wyckoff, *A History of the 2nd South Carolina Infantry: 1861–65* (Fredericksburg, Va.: Sergeant Kirkland: Museum and Historical Society, Inc., 1994), viii–xiii. The other company names were: Company B—Butler Guards; Company D—Sumter Volunteers; Company E—Camden Volunteers; Company F—Secession Guards; Company G—Flat Rock Guards; Company H—Lancaster Invincibles; Company I—Palmetto Guards; Company K—Brooks Guards.

11. Warner, *Generals in Gray,* 170–71; Busey and Martin, *Regimental Strengths and Losses,* 138.

12. Crute, *Units of the Confederate States Army,* 252; Mac Wyckoff, *A History of the 3rd South Carolina Infantry 1861–1865* (Fredericksburg, Va.: Sergeant Kirkland's Museum and History Society, Inc., 1995), 7–10. The company names were: Company A—State Guards; Company B—Williams Guards; Company C—Pickens Guards; Company D—Cross Anchors; Company E—Quitman Rifles; Company G—Laurens Briars; Company I—Musgrove Volunteers; Company K—Blackstock.

13. Wyckoff, *History of the 3rd South Carolina,* 11; Robert K. Krick, *Lee's Colonels: A Biographical Register of the Field Officers of the Army of Northern Virginia,* 4th ed. (Dayton, Ohio: Morningside House, Inc. 1992), 287, 399; Mac Wyckoff, "Kershaw's Brigade at Gettysburg," *Gettysburg Magazine,* (July 1991), 35; Busey and Martin, *Regimental Strengths and Losses,* 138.

14. Crute, *Units of the Confederate States Army,* 255–56; D. Augustus Dickert, *History of Kershaw's Brigade with Complete Roll of Companies, Biographical Sketches, Incidents, Anecdotes, Etc.* (Dayton, Ohio: Morningside Bookshop, 1988), 37–38; Krick, *Lee's Colonels,* 30–31, 40; Busey and Martin, *Regimental Strengths and Losses,* 138.

15. Dickert, *History of Kershaw's Brigade,* 38–39; Krick, *Lee's Colonels,* 88, 189; Busey and Martin, *Regimental Strengths and Losses,* 138.

16. Crute, *Units of the Confederate States Army,* 260; Busey and Martin, *Regimental Strengths and Losses,* 138; Krick, *Lee's Colonels,* 118–19.

17. Dickert, *History of Kershaw's Brigade,* 250–51.

18. Busey and Martin, *Regimental Strengths and Losses,* 138; Crute, *Units of the Confederate States Army,* 251–52; Dickert, *History of Kershaw's Brigade,* 171–72.

19. Krick, *Lee's Colonels,* 207, 318; Dickert, *History of Kershaw's Brigade,* 313–14.

20. Biographical information on Paul J. Semmes in Warner, *Generals in Gray,* 272–73; Andrew Humphreys, *Semmes America* (Memphis, Tenn.: Humphreys Ink, Inc., 1989), 387–88.

21. Humphreys, *Semmes America,* 388.

22. June 23, 1863, letter of Paul Semmes, in Gary Kross, "To Die Like Soldiers...The Retreat from Sickles' Front, July 2, 1863," *Blue & Gray* Magazine, vol. 15, issue 5, 21.

23. Busey and Martin, *Regimental Strengths and Losses,* 140; Crute, *Units of the Confederate States Army,* 91; Warner, *Generals in Gray,* 66.

24. Krick, *Lee's Colonels,* 390.

25. John Griffin, *Warriors of the Wiregrass* (Moultrie, Ga.: private printing, 2000). Company names were: Company B—Ware Volunteers (Ware County); Company

C—Coffee Guards (Coffee County); Company D—Valdasta Guards (Lowndes County); Company E—Thomas County Rangers; Company F—Decatur Infantry (DeKalb County); Company G—Clinch Volunteers (Clinch County); Company I—Berrien Light Infantry (Berrien County); and Company K—Brooks Volunteers (Brooks and Fayette Counties).

26. Krick, *Lee's Colonels*, 262; Busey and Martin, *Regimental Strengths and Losses*, 140.

27. Busey and Martin, *Regimental Strengths and Losses*, 140; Crute, *Units of the Confederate States Army*, 112. The remaining company names were: Company C—Mitchell Van Guards (Mitchell County); Company D—Miller Guards (Baker, Colquitt, and Miller Counties); Company E—Pochitta Guards (Baker and Calhoun Counties); Company F—Terrell Infantry (Terrell County); Company G—Harrison Volunteers (Quitman County); Company H—Randolph Rangers (Randolph County); Company I—Clay Volunteers (Clay County); and Company K—Dougherty Grays (Dougherty County).

28. Krick, *Lee's Colonels*, 43–44, 348.

29. Krick, *Lee's Colonels*, 122–23; Warner, *Generals in Gray*, 277–78; Welsch, *Medical Histories of Confederate Generals*, 197.

30. Biographical information on William T. Wofford in Warner, *Generals in Gray*, 343–44; Gerald J. Smith, *"One of the Most Daring of Men": The Life of Confederate General William Tatum Wofford* (Murfreesboro, Tenn.: Southern Heritage Press, 1997), 1–65.

31. Clement A. Evans, ed., *Confederate Military History*, vol. 7, 38–39; Crute, *Units of the Confederate States Army*, 95–96; Warner, *Generals in Gray*, 55.

32. Warner, *Generals in Gray*, 37; Sifakis, *Who Was Who in the Civil War*, 83; Busey and Martin, *Regimental Strengths and Losses*, 141.

33. Krick, *Lee's Colonels*, 328; Sifakis, *Who Was Who in the Civil War*, 558; Busey and Martin, *Regimental Strengths and Losses*, 141. The regiment was formed in the spring of 1861, with men from Cobb, Dooly, Jackson, Newton, and Stephens Counties; Crute, *Units of the Confederate States Army*, 96.

34. The company names were: Company A—Independent Volunteers; Company C—White County Marksmen; Company D—Hiawassee Volunteers; Company E—Rabun Gap Riflemen; Company F—Gwinnett Independent Blues; Company H—Currahee Rangers; Company I—Glade Guards Volunteer Rifles; and Company K—McMillan Guards.

35. Crute, *Units of the Confederate States Army*, 100–101; Krick, *Lee's Colonels*, 256.

36. The Cobb Legion had seven companies of infantry, four of cavalry, and one of artillery. Only the infantry regiment served in Wofford's Brigade. Evans, *Confederate Military History*, 7:35; Warner, *Generals in Gray*, 56; Krick, *Lee's Colonels*, 158; Busey and Martin, *Regimental Strengths and Losses*, 141.

37. Evans, *Confederate Military History*, 7:35; Crute, *Units of the Confederate States Army*, 120–21; Krick, *Lee's Colonels*, 46.

Chapter Two

1. *OR*, vol. 27, pt. 2, 293.

2. Ibid., 305.

3. Ibid., 306.

4. Ibid., 357.

5. Ibid., 358.

6. Lafayette McLaws, "Gettysburg," *SHSP* (Dayton, Ohio: Broadfoot Publishing Company/Morningside House, 1990), vol. 7, 65.

7. Guy R. Everson and Edward H. Simpson, Jr., eds., *"Far, Far from Home": The Wartime Letters of Dick and Tally Simpson, 3rd South Carolina Volunteers* (New York: Oxford University Press, 1994), 249.

8. Franklin Gaillard to son, June 28, 1863. Franklin Gaillard Collection #3790, Southern Historical Society Collection, University of North Carolina, Chapel Hill, 33.

9. *OR*, vol. 27, pt. 2, 366; Gaillard, 32.

10. *OR*, vol. 27, pt. 2, 371.

11. Mac Wyckoff, "Kershaw's Brigade at Gettysburg," 38; *OR*, vol. 27, pt. 2, 371.

12. *OR*, vol. 27, pt. 2, 366, 371; Wyckoff, "Kershaw's Brigade at Gettysburg," 38.

13. Everson and Simpson, *Far, Far, from Home*, 249.

14. Dickert, *History of Kershaw's Brigade*, 229.

15. L. L. Cochran, "Some Incidents on the March to Gettysburg," *Atlanta Journal*, August 31, 1901.

16. McLaws, "Gettysburg," *SHSP*, vol. 7, 65–66.

17. *OR*, vol. 27, pt. 3, 912–13.

18. Edwin B. Coddington, *The Gettysburg Campaign: A Study in Command* (New York: Charles Scribner's Sons, 1979), 153–58.

19. Simpson, *Far, Far from Home*, 251.

20. Ibid., 262.

21. Gaillard, 34.

22. Cochran, "Some Incidents on the March to Gettysburg," *Atlanta Journal*, August 31, 1901.

23. Gaillard, 34.

24. *OR*, vol. 27, pt. 2, 366, 371.

25. Diary of Marcus Green, Kennesaw Mountain National Military Park, 6.

26. Smith, *One of the Most Daring of Men*, 80.

27. McLaws, "Gettysburg," *SHSP*, vol. 7, 67.

28. John Coxe, "The Battle of Gettysburg," *Confederate Veteran* (Wilmington, N.C.: Broadfoot Publishing Company, 1987, 1988, reprint), vol. 21, no. 9, (1913), 433.

29. Ibid.

30. McLaws, "Gettysburg," *SHSP*, vol. 7, 67–68; Coxe, "The Battle of Gettysburg," 433; Harry W. Pfanz, *Gettysburg: The Second Day* (Chapel Hill and London: The University of North Carolina Press, 1987), 24.

31. James Longstreet, "Lee in Pennsylvania," *The Annals of the War Written by Leading Participants North and South* (originally published in the *Philadelphia Weekly Times*, reprint Dayton, Ohio: Morningside House, 1988), 421.

32. John A. Everett to his mother, June 21, 1863, File #58, letter #8, Emory University Special Collections.

33. Samuel Brewer letter, June 11, 1863, in Candler H. Thaxton, *My Dear Wife from Your Devoted Husband: Letters from a Rebel Soldier to his Wife* (Warringtown, Fla.: privately printed, 1968).

34. George Hillyer, "Battle of Gettysburg," Address Before the Walton County Georgia Confederate Veterans, August 2, 1904.

35. Coddington, *The Gettysburg Campaign*, 370–71; John B. Hood, *Advance and Retreat: Personal Experiences in the United States and Confederate States Armies* (New Orleans: n.p. 1880), 57.

36. Johnston to McLaws, June 27, 1892, Lafayette McLaws Papers, Duke University.

37. Ibid.

38. *OR*, vol. 27, pt. 2, 366; Joseph Kershaw, "Kershaw's Brigade at Gettysburg," Robert U. Johnson and Clarence C. Buel, eds., *Battles and Leaders of the Civil War*, 4 vols. (New York: Century Company, 1884–1889; New York: Castle Books, 1956), 3:331.

39. McLaws, "Gettysburg," *SHSP*, vol. 7, 68.

40. Pfanz, *Gettysburg: The Second Day*, 119; McLaws, "Gettysburg," *SHSP*, vol. 7, 69.

41. William M. Abernathy, *Our Mess: Southern Gallantry and Privations* (McKinney, Tex.: McKintex Press, 1977), 31.

42. Gary W. Gallagher, ed., *Fighting for the Confederacy: The Personal Recollections of General Edward Porter Alexander* (Chapel Hill/London: The University of North Carolina Press, 1989), 235–36. [Author's note: Alexander mentions that he turned out to the "left" near the hill, but it had to have been a turn to the right instead.]

43. Ibid.

44. McLaws, "Gettysburg," *SHSP*, vol. 7, 69.

45. Ibid.

46. Dickert, *History of Kershaw's Brigade*, 235–36.

47. Ibid.

48. Pfanz, *Gettysburg: The Second Day*, 120–21; McLaws "Gettysburg," *SHSP*, vol. 7, 69.

49. McLaws, "Gettysburg," *SHSP*, vol. 7, 69.

Chapter Three

1. McLaws, "Gettysburg," *SHSP*, vol. 7, 70; Pfanz, *Gettysburg: The Second Day*, 120–23; Kershaw, "Kershaw's Brigade at Gettysburg," 332; Wyckoff, *The 3rd South Carolina Infantry*, 118–20.

2. E. P. Alexander, "The Great Charge and Artillery Fighting at Gettysburg," *Battles and Leaders of the Civil War*, 3:360; Kershaw, "Kershaw's Brigade at Gettysburg," 332; McLaws, "Gettysburg," *SHSP*, vol. 7, 70; John Bachelder Map, July 2, 1863; Pfanz, *Gettysburg: The Second Day*, 497; Smith, *One of the Most Daring of Men*, 81.

3. Evander M. Law, "The Struggle for Round Top," *Battles and Leaders of the Civil War*, 3:320; John Purifoy, "Longstreet's Attack at Gettysburg, July 2, 1863," *Confederate Veteran* 31 (1923): 292; Pfanz, *Gettysburg: The Second Day*, 159–60; *OR*, vol. 27, pt. 1, 396–97.

4. Kershaw, "Kershaw's Brigade at Gettysburg," 333–34.

5. Ezra J. Warner, *Generals in Blue: Lives of the Union Commanders* (Baton Rouge and London: Louisiana State University Press, 1991), 446–47.

6. Pfanz, *Gettysburg: The Second Day*, 97–101; Ray Marcot, "Berdan Sharpshooters at Gettysburg," *Historical Articles of Lasting Interest* (July 1989): 35–40.

7. For a detailed analysis of the Meade-Sickles controversy, see Richard A. Sauers, *A Caspian Sea of Ink: The Meade-Sickles Controversy* (Baltimore: Butternut and Blue, 1989).

8. Pfanz, *Gettysburg: The Second Day*, 133–34, 307, 311–12.

9. Ibid., 127–29.

10. John B. Bachelder Map, 4 P.M., July 2, 1863.

11. McLaws, "Gettysburg," *SHSP*, vol. 7, 72–73.

12. George Hillyer, "Battle of Gettysburg," Address Before the Walton County Georgia Confederate Veterans, August 2, 1904, Walton *Tribune*, 5.

13. George T. Anderson to John B. Bachelder, December 4, 1894, *The Bachelder Papers: Gettysburg in Their Own Words*, 3 vols. (Dayton, Ohio: Morningside, 1994–1995).

Chapter Four

1. *OR*, vol. 27, pt. 2, 405.

2. Travis Hudson, "Soldier Boys in Gray: A History of the 59th Georgia Volunteer Infantry Regiment," *Atlanta Journal*, vol. 23, no. 1 (Spring 1979): 56.

3. Hillyer, "Battle of Gettysburg," 5–6.

4. *OR*, vol. 27, pt. 2, 399; Pfanz, *Gettysburg: The Second Day*, 175–76, 247; Gary Kross, "Rebel Yells on Both Flanks," *Blue & Gray* Magazine 5 (March 1988), 24; Diary of J. C. Reid, 69, Alabama State Archives.

5. July 18, 1863, letter from John and Tom Mounger to Mrs. John C. Mounger found in State of Georgia Archives, reel #2241.

6. May 23, 1863, letter from John C. Mounger to his wife, Lucie; *Atlanta Journal*, Winter 1982–1983, 23.

7. *OR*, vol. 27, pt. 1, 506, 513.

8. Erasmus Gilbreath Collection, Indiana State Library, Collection S2594, 71, 72.

9. Ibid.

10. Ibid., 72.

11. *OR*, vol. 27, pt. 2, 407.

12. *OR*, vol. 27, pt. 2, 403, 407.

13. *OR*, vol. 27, pt. 2, 403; Erasmus Gilbreath, 73.

14. *OR*, vol. 27, pt. 2, 401.

15. Diary of Lt. J. C. Reid, Alabama State Archives, Montgomery, Ala.

16. Ibid.

17. Hillyer, "Battle of Gettysburg," 6.

18. Pennsylvania Gettysburg Battlefield Commission, *Pennsylvania at Gettysburg: Ceremonies at the Dedication of the Monuments Erected by the Commonwealth of Pennsylvania to Mark the Positions of the Pennsylvania Commands Engaged in the Battle,* John P. Nicholson, ed., 2 vols. (Harrisburg, Pa.: W. S. Ray, State Printer, 1904), 2:589–90; James C. M. Hamilton, "History of the 110th Pennsylvania Infantry Regiment," Military Order of the Loyal Legion of the U.S. Collection, Civil War Library and Museum, Philadelphia, Pa., 121; James C. Hamilton, "The 110th Pennsylvania in the Gettysburg Campaign," *Philadelphia Weekly Press*, February 24, 1886.

19. Gregory A. Coco, *Killed in Action: Eyewitness Accounts of the Last Moments of 100 Union Soldiers Who Died at Gettysburg* (Gettysburg, Pa.: Thomas Publications, 1992), 48–49.

20. Hamilton, "History of the 110th Pennsylvania Infantry Regiment," 124; *OR*, vol. 27, pt. 1, 528–29.

21. Tagg, *The Generals of Gettysburg*, 79–80.

22. Janet B. Hewett, Noah Andre Trudeau, and Bryce A. Suderow, eds., *Supplement to the Official Records of the Union and Confederate Armies* (Wilmington, N.C.: Broadfoot Publishing Company, 1995), vol. 5, 185.

23. Ibid.

24. *OR*, vol. 27, pt. 1, 522; John Haley to John B. Bachelder, *The Bachelder Papers*, 836–40, 994–99, 1008–10; George W. Verrill to John E. Bachelder, *The Bachelder Papers*, 1010–15, 1035–39, 1058–60, 1063–67; *OR*, vol. 27, pt. 1, 570–71.

25. Ken Bandy and Florence Freeland, comps., *The Gettysburg Papers Volume II* (Dayton, Ohio: Morningside Bookshop, 1986), 592–93; William Barnes Jordan, Jr.,

Red Diamond Regiment: The 17th Maine Infantry, 1862–1865 (Shippensburg, Pa.: White Mane Publishing Company, Inc., 1996), 74; John P. Dunne to John B. Bachelder, *The Bachelder Papers*, 1052.

26. Toombs, *New Jersey Troops in the Gettysburg Campaign*, 219.

27. Martin and Busey, *Regimental Strengths and Losses at Gettysburg*, 247; John P. Dunne to John B. Bachelder, *The Bachelder Papers*, 1050–52; Toombs, *New Jersey Troops in the Gettysburg Campaign*, 219. Among the losses was Col. John Ramsey of the 8th New Jersey, who was wounded in the shoulders.

28. Daniel Gookin Journal, Lewis Leigh Collection, US Army Military History Institute, Book 8 #39; *OR*, vol. 27, pt. 1, 522; Bandy and Freeland, *The Gettysburg Papers, Vol. II*, 593.

29. Charles W. Roberts, "At Gettysburg in 1863 and 1888," *The Gettysburg Papers*, 593. Verrill's account of the movement was as follows: "The three right companies and part of the fourth thus formed the flanking line along a rail fence which joined the stone wall at about a right angle and was the boundary of the real Wheatfield at the west. The alder growth was now about fifty yards in front of his flank line, leaving a fine roadway between; the rest of the regiment remained of course where they were at the wall." *The Gettysburg Papers*, 566.

30. Pfanz, *Gettysburg: The Second Day*, 251.

31. John Haley, *What I saw at Gettysburg July 2 & 3, 1863*, private journal from collection of Stan Domosh, N.J., 6.

32. Verrill, "The Seventeenth Maine at Gettysburg and in the Wilderness," 573.

33. *OR*, vol. 27, pt. 2, 401.

34. Warner, *Generals in Blue*, 492–93; Tagg, *The Generals of Gettysburg*, 81–83.

35. Warner, *Generals in Blue*, 20–21; Tagg, *The Generals of Gettysburg*, 83–85.

36. Tagg, *The Generals of Gettysburg*, 86–89.

37. John B. Bachelder Maps, July 2, 1863, 4 P.M.; James Houghton Journal, Michigan Historical Collection, Bentley Historical Library, University of Michigan.

38. Oscar W. West, "On Little Round Tops The Fifth Corps Fight at Gettysburg Particularly the 32d Mass.'s Part," in Richard A. Sauers, ed., *Fighting Them Over How the Veterans Remembered Gettysburg in the Pages of the National Tribune* (Baltimore, Md.: Butternut and Blue, 1998), 295.

39. Busey and Martin, *Regimental Strengths and Losses*, 59; *OR*, vol. 27, pt. 1, 607. Tilton's report describes the position of his brigade on Stony Hill:

    in a piece of woods at the south of Mr. Rose's house. The Second Brigade was on our left, but there being no infantry upon our right, I made a crotchet by refusing the right wing of my right battalion (118th PA). The line was like

2d Brigade	22d Mass.	1st Mich.	118th Penn.	Rose's House
	18th Mass	118 PA		

40. Colonel J. B. Sweitzer's account from Joshua L. Chamberlain Papers, Library of Congress; Busey and Martin, *Regimental Strengths and Losses*, 60.

41. *OR*, vol. 27, pt. 1, 610–11.

42. *OR*, vol. 27, pt. 1, 611.

43. *OR*, vol. 27, pt. 1, 607–8; Colonel J. B. Sweitzer's account from Joshua L. Chamberlain Papers, Library of Congress (photocopy in Gettysburg National Military Park Library, Vertical Files).

44. Pfanz, *Gettysburg The Second Day*, 245; Busey and Martin, *Regimental Strengths and Losses*, 247–48.

Chapter Five

1. Verrill, "The Seventeenth Maine at Gettysburg and in the Wilderness," 573; Regis de Trobriand, *Four Years with the Army of the Potomac* (Gaithersburg, Md.: Ron R. Van Sickle Military Books, 1988), 497.

2. Anderson to Bachelder, March 15, 1876, and December 4, 1894, *The Bachelder Papers,* 449–50, 1871.

3. Gallagher, ed., *Fighting for the Confederacy,* 239.

4. Kershaw, "Kershaw's Brigade at Gettysburg," 334.

5. Ibid., 335; *OR,* vol. 27, pt. 2, 367–68.

6. Coxe, "The Battle of Gettysburg," 434.

7. *OR,* vol. 27, pt. 2, 368.

8. Pfanz, *Gettysburg: The Second Day,* 315; Michael Hanifer, *History of Battery B, First New Jersey Artillery* (Cottawa, Ill.: Republican Times Printers, 1905), 74–75.

9. Wyckoff, *A History of the 2nd South Carolina Infantry 1861–1865,* 80; William Johnson, "Gettysburg," *Atlanta Journal,* date and page unknown in files at Fredericksburg and Spotsylvania National Military Park.

10. *OR,* vol. 27, pt. 2, 368.

11. Kershaw, "Kershaw's Brigade at Gettysburg," 335.

12. Gaillard, 36.

13. William T. Shumate, "With Kershaw at Gettysburg," *Philadelphia Times Weekly,* May, 1882. p. unknown.

14. Shumate also experienced a moment of levity at the expense of his adjutant, Edward E. Sill. Sill was near Shumate when he was painfully wounded in the foot with a grape or canister shot. He asked Shumate to help him by cutting off the boot from the wounded foot, which Shumate did. Sill then rose, and with a quick glance at the Union battery, ran as fast as his bloodied, bootless foot could take him to safety, with no further thought of fighting the enemy that day. Ibid.

15. Eric Campbell, "Baptism of Fire: The Ninth Massachusetts Battery at Gettysburg, July 2, 1863," *Gettysburg Magazine* (July 1991): 62–63; John Bigelow, *The Peach Orchard: Gettysburg, July 2, 1863* (Gaithersburg, Md.: Olde Soldier Books, Inc., 1987), 21, 54–56.

16. *Pennsylvania at Gettysburg,* vol. 2, 634; Survivors' Association, *History of the Corn Exchange Regiment, 118th Pennsylvania Volunteers* (Philadelphia: J. L. Smith, 1888), 244.

17. Anderson to Bachelder, March 15, 1876, *The Bachelder Papers,* 1:449–50; Kershaw, "Kershaw's Brigade at Gettysburg," 336.

18. John L. Smith Papers, 118th Pennsylvania Regiment, letter to Mother, July 9, 1863, Historical Society of Pennsylvania, Philadelphia, Pennsylvania.

19. J. Gregory Acken, ed., *Inside the Army of the Potomac: The Civil War Experience of Captain Francis Adams Donaldson* (Mechanicsburg, Pa.: Stackpole Books, 1998), 303.

20. John L. Parker, *Henry Wilson's Regiment: History of the Twenty-Second Massachusetts Infantry, the Second Company Sharpshooters, and the Third Light Battery, in the War of the Rebellion* (Baltimore, Md.: Butternut and Blue, 1996), 334.

21. *OR,* vol. 27, pt. 1, 607–8.

22. *Pennsylvania at Gettysburg,* vol. 2, 634.

23. Ibid.

24. Acken, *Inside the Army of the Potomac,* 303–4; John L. Smith Papers, July 9, 1863, letter to Mother.

25. Acken, *Inside the Army of the Potomac*, 305.

26. Parker, *Henry Wilson's Regiment*, 335; *OR*, vol. 27, pt. 1, 607–8.

27. John Robertson, ed., *Michigan in the War* (Lansing, Mich.: George, 1882), 179.

28. *OR*, vol. 27, pt. 1, 601.

29. Ibid., 611.

30. *OR*, vol. 27, pt. 1, 611; Col. J. B. Sweitzer's account from Joshua L. Chamberlain Papers, Library of Congress; Martin Bertera and Ken Oberholtzer, *The 4th Michigan Volunteer Infantry at Gettysburg: The Battle for the Wheatfield* (Dayton, Ohio: Morningside House, Inc., 1997), 68–72.

31. James Houghton Journal, Gettysburg National Military Park Library, 13.

32. John Milton Bancroft Journal, July 2, 1863, Michigan Historical Collection.

33. *Pennsylvania at Gettysburg*, 383; Hull to Bachelder, *The Bachelder Papers*, 110–11.

34. John Bigelow, *The Peach Orchard: Gettysburg, July 2, 1863* (Gaithersburg, Md.: Olde Soldier Books, Inc., 1987), 55–56.

35. *OR*, vol. 27, pt. 1, 520.

36. de Trobriand, *Four Years with the Army of the Potomac*, 499; William B. Styple, ed., *Our Noble Blood: The Civil War Letters of Major-General Regis de Trobriand* (Kearny, N.J.: Belle Grove Publishing Co., 1997), 116; *OR*, vol. 27, pt. 1, 520.

37. de Trobriand, *Four Years with the Army of the Potomac*, 500.

38. Franklin I. Whitmore, July 5, 1863, letter, Personal Collection of Steve Zerbe, Cherry Hill, New Jersey.

39. Haley to Bachelder, February 2, 1884, letter, *The Bachelder Papers*, 996.

40. *OR*, vol. 27, pt. 1, 587.

41. Pfanz, *Gettysburg: The Second Day*, 262–64; *OR*, vol. 27, pt. 1, 587.

42. John Haley, *What I saw at Gettysburg July 2 & 3, 1863*, Sacco, Maine, 11–12, Private Collection of Stan Domash, N.J.

43. Verrill to Merrill, February 11, 1884, letter, *The Bachelder Papers*, 1014; George W. Verrill, "The Seventeenth Maine at Gettysburg and in the Wilderness," Ken Bandy and Florence Freeland, comps., *The Gettysburg Papers Vol. II* (Dayton, Ohio: Morningside Bookshop, 1986), 574–75; Charles W. Roberts, "At Gettysburg in 1863 and 1888," *The Gettysburg Papers, Vol. II*, 594–95; *OR*, vol. 27, pt. 1, 522; Edward B. Houghton, *The Campaigns of the Seventeenth Maine* (Portland, Maine: Short & Loring, 1866), 98–99.

44. Kershaw, "Kershaw's Brigade at Gettysburg," 336.

45. Ibid.; *OR*, vol. 27, pt. 2, 368.

46. Cochran, "The Tenth Georgia Regiment at Gettysburg," *Atlanta Journal*, February 23, 1901.

47. Humphrey, *Semmes America*, 393–95.

48. Ibid.

49. Ibid.

50. Ibid.

51. Warner, *Generals in Blue*, 63–64; Tagg, *The Generals of Gettysburg*, 35–36.

52. Charles A. Hale, "With Colonel Cross in the Gettysburg Campaign," Miscellaneous Papers, John Rutter Brooke Papers, Historical Society of Pennsylvania, Philadelphia, Pa., viii.

53. Bachelder Maps, July 2, 1863, 4 P.M.; Hale, "With Colonel Cross in the Gettysburg Campaign," viii.

54. Letter from Reverend William Corby to John Bachelder, January 4, 1879, Historian's Office, Gettysburg National Military Park.

55. Ibid.; Kevin E. O'Brien, "Into the Wheatfield: The Union Army's Irish Brigade at Gettysburg," Vertical Files, Gettysburg National Military Park, 10–14.

56. A. M. Gambone, *The Life of General Samuel K. Zook: Another Forgotten Union Hero* (Baltimore, Md.: Butternut and Blue, 1996), 9–12; Henry Edwin Tremain, *Two Days of War: A Gettysburg Narrative and other Excursions* (New York: Bonnell, Silvers and Bowers, 1905), 81–87.

57. *OR*, vol. 27, pt. 1, 400.

58. Hale, "With Colonel Cross in the Gettysburg Campaign," viii.

59. Obituary for Edward E. Cross, *Coos Democrat*; Larry Tagg, *The Generals of Gettysburg*, 37–38.

60. D. Scott Hartwig, "No Troops on the Field Had Done Better": John C. Caldwell's Division in the Wheatfield, July 2, 1863," in Gary Gallagher, ed., *The Second Day at Gettysburg: Essays on Confederate and Union Leadership* (Kent, Ohio: The Kent State University Press, 1993), 151–52; Eric Campbell, "Caldwell Clears the Wheatfield," *Gettysburg Magazine* (July 1990): 35; Hale, "With Colonel Cross in the Gettysburg Campaign," xii–xiii.

61. Hartwig, "Caldwell's Division in the Wheatfield," 151–59; Campbell, "Caldwell Clears the Wheatfield," 39–41.

62. *OR*, vol. 27, pt. 1, 381–82; Muffly, *148th Pennsylvania*, 537.

63. Charles A. Fuller, *Personal Recollections of the War of 1861* (Hamilton, N.Y.: Edmonston Publishing, Inc., reprint, 1990), 93–98; *OR*, vol. 27, pt. 1, 384.

64. Ezra J. Warner, *Generals in Blue*, 576–77; Tagg, *The Generals of Gettysburg*, 40–42; *Memorial to Samuel K. Zook* (Philadelphia, Pa.: James Beale, printer, 1889), pp. 16–17; Gambone, *The Life of General Samuel K. Zook: Another Forgotten Union Hero*, 14–21.

65. Josiah Marshall Favill, *The Diary of a Young Officer Serving with the Armies of the United States during the War of the Rebellion* (Chicago: R. R. Donnelly & Sons Company, 1909), 246.

66. Jacob H. Cole, *Under Five Commanders or A Boy's Experience with the Army of the Potomac* (Paterson, N.J.: News Printing Company, 1906), 202–3.

67. George Meade, *The Life and Letters of George Gordon Meade*, 2 vols. (New York: Charles Scribner's Sons, 1913), vol. 2, 327–28.

68. "St. Louisians among Gettysburg Heroes," St. Louis *Globe-Democrat*, March 9, 1912, 15, col. 1.

69. Pfanz, *Gettysburg: The Second Day*, 275.

70. *OR*, vol. 27, pt. 1, 394; Robert L. Stewart, *History of the One Hundred and Fortieth Regiment* (———, Pa.: Regimental Association, 1912), 104; Sara Gould Walters, *Inscription at Gettysburg* (Gettysburg, Pa.: Thomas Publications, 1991), 106–8.

71. William Shallenberger to John Bachelder, *The Bachelder Papers*, 1578; Walters, *Inscription at Gettysburg*, 108.

72. Gaillard, 36.

73. Hartwig, "Caldwell's Division in the Wheatfield," 152–59; Campbell, "Caldwell Clears the Wheatfield," 39–41.

74. Kevin E. O'Brien, "Into the Wheatfield: The Union Army's Irish Brigade at Gettysburg," 4; Stewart Sifakis, *Who Was Who in the Civil War* (New York and Oxford: Facts on File Publications, 1988), 358; Tagg, *The Generals of Gettysburg*, 39–40.

75. David Wyatt Aiken, "The Gettysburg Reunion. What is Necessary and Proper for the South to Do. Open Letter from Col. D. Wyatt Aiken to Gen. J. B. Kershaw," *Charleston News and Courier*, June 21, 1882.

76. *New York at Gettysburg*, 479; *OR*, vol. 27, pt. 1, 387–89.

77. Kershaw, "Kershaw Brigade at Gettysburg," 336–37; Kershaw to Bachelder letter, dated March 20, 1876, *The Bachelder Papers*, 456; Pfanz, *Gettysburg: The Second Day*, 281–82.

78. *OR*, vol. 27, pt. 2, 372.

79. Tagg, *The Generals of Gettysburg*, 42–44; Warner, *Generals in Blue*, 46–47; *OR*, vol. 27, pt. 1, 380–81.

80. "B. J. Worden's Gettysburg Experience," Indiana Division, Indiana State Library, Collection S1361.

81. *OR*, vol. 27, pt. 1, 406; Pfanz, *Gettysburg: The Second Day*, 284; *OR* Supplement, vol. 5, 155; Winthrop D. Sheldon, *The "Twenty-Seventh": A Regimental History* (New Haven: Morris & Benham, 1866), 77; *OR*, vol. 27, pt. 2, 372.

82. Martin Sigman Diary, U.S. History mss., Manuscript Department, Lilly Library, Indiana University, Bloomington, Ind., 51; Brooke to Bachelder, March 18, 1886, *The Bachelder Papers*, 1234; *OR*, vol. 27, pt. 1, 400.

83. *OR*, vol. 27, pt. 1, 409, 422; Pfanz, *Gettysburg: The Second Day*, 286.

84. Sheldon, *The "Twenty-Seventh": A Regimental History*, 77.

85. Cochran, "Some Incidents on the March to Gettysburg."

86. Griffin, *Warriors of the Wiregrass*, 276.

87. "A Yankee at Gettysburg," *National Tribune*, October 10, 1918; Sheldon, *The "Twenty-Seventh": A Regimental History*, 77.

88. Hartwig, "Caldwell's Division in the Wheatfield," 162–63; Campbell, "Caldwell Clears the Wheatfield," 45–47; Brooke to Walker, March 18, 1886, letter, *The Bachelder Papers*, 1233–34.

89. *OR*, vol. 27, pt. 1, 403; Brooke to Walker, November 14, 1885, letter, *The Bachelder Papers*, 1139–43.

Chapter Six

1. McLaws, "Gettysburg," *SHSP*, vol. 7, 74.

2. John Alexander Barry Papers, Barry letter, July 8, 1863, Southern Historical Collection—University of North Carolina, C#3015–2, Folder #2; Royall W. Figg, *"Where Men Only Dare to Go!": On the Story of a Boy Company by an Ex-Boy* (Richmond: Whittet and Shepperson, 1885), 140.

3. *Richmond Sentinel*, July 27, 1863.

4. William Youngblood, "Personal Observations at Gettysburg," *Confederate Veteran*, vol. 19, 286; Bryan to McLaws letter, December 10, 1877, Southern Historical Collection, University of North Carolina.

5. *OR*, vol. 27, pt. 2, 369.

6. Coxe, "The Battle of Gettysburg," *Confederate Veteran*, vol. 21, 434.

7. Ibid., 435.

8. *OR*, vol. 27, pt. 1, 395.

9. *Pennsylvania at Gettysburg*, 684.

10. Gregory A. Coco, *On the Bloodstained Field* (Gettysburg, Pa.: Thomas Publications, 1987), 21.

11. *The Bachelder Papers*, 418.

12. Thomas Blackburn Rodgers, "St. Louisians among Gettysburg Heroes," *Globe-Democrat*, March 9, 1913, 15.

13. *New York at Gettysburg*, 420.

14. *OR*, vol. 27, pt. 1, 397.

15. *OR*, vol. 27, pt. 1, 398.

16. Richard Coffman, "A Vital Unit," *Civil War Times Illustrated*, 20 (June 1982), 44.

17. John Alexander Barry, July 8, 1863, letter, Southern Historical Collection, University of North Carolina.

18. Warner, *Generals in Blue*, 13–14; Tagg, *The Generals of Gettysburg*, 91–93.

19. *OR*, vol. 27, pt. 1, 379, 602, 611, 634–35.

20. *OR*, vol. 27, pt. 1, 612.

21. *OR*, vol. 27, pt. 1, 400–401, 611–12.

22. Colonel J. B. Sweitzer's Account from Joshua L. Chamberlain Papers, Library of Congress.

23. Francis J. Parker, *The Story of the Thirty-Second Regiment Massachusetts Infantry* (Boston: C. W. Calkins & Co., 1880), 170–71; Oscar W. West, "On Little Round Top," *The National Tribune*, November 22, 1906.

24. *Richmond Daily Enquirer*, August 5, 1863.

25. Robert Campbell, "Pioneer Memories of the War Days 1861–1865," 30 *Michigan Pioneer and Historical Collections* (1906), 569; Kathy George Harrison, August 15, 1987, letter to Don Troiani, Gettysburg National Military Park; Lt. Col. James C. Hull, March 24, 1864, letter, *The Bachelder Papers*, 111; Henry S. Seage, September 23, 1884, letter, *The Bachelder Papers*, 1070–72; James Houghton Journal, 14, Michigan Historical Collection, Bentley Historical Library, University of Michigan; *Michigan at Gettysburg: Proceedings Incident to the Dedication of the Michigan Monuments upon the Battlefield of Gettysburg, June 12, 1889* (Detroit, Mich.: Winn & Hammon, 1889), 85–86. Jeffords' last words were "Mother, mother, mother." The colonel could certainly have used the six-barreled, self-cocking revolver that he had carried throughout the war; yet, just the day before, he had presented it to Robert Campbell, his old high-school classmate serving as quartermaster for the 4th Michigan. Robert Campbell account, Michigan Historical Collection, Bentley Historical Library, University of Michigan.

26. George W. Whipple, "Memories of George W. Whipple," 21, Typescript, Fredericksburg and Spotsylvania National Military Park.

27. *OR*, vol. 27, pt. 1, 401.

28. *OR*, vol. 27, pt. 1, 379–80, 645; Kross, "To Die Like Soldiers", 19.

29. Tagg, *The Generals of Gettysburg*, 93–94.

30. Ibid., 94–95.

31. *OR*, vol. 27, pt. 1, 612.

32. *OR*, vol. 27, pt. 1, 645.

33. *OR*, vol. 27, pt. 1, 643.

34. William H. Powell, *The Fifth Army Corps, Army of the Potomac* (Dayton, Ohio: Morningside Bookshop, 1984), 534–35.

35. *OR*, vol. 27, pt. 1, 646.

36. Ibid.

37. *OR*, vol. 27, pt. 1, 647–48.

38. *OR*, vol. 27, pt. 1, 648–51; Timothy J. Reese, *Sykes' Regular Infantry Division, 1861–1864* (Jefferson, N.C., and London: McFarland & Company, Inc., 1990), 250–51.

39. Powell, *The Fifth Army Corps*, 535.

40. *OR*, vol. 27, pt. 1, 662; Pfanz, *Gettysburg: The Second Day*, 395.

41. *OR*, vol. 27, pt. 1, 662.

42. Powell, *The Fifth Corps*, 535.

43. Kross, "To Die Like Soldiers," 23; Reese, *Sykes' Regulars Infantry Division, 1861–1864*, 253.

44. Richard Robins, "The Regular Troops at Gettysburg," *Philadelphia Weekly Times*, vol. 2, no. 45 (January 4, 1879), 1.

45. Kershaw, "Kershaw's Brigade at Gettysburg," 337; Wyckoff, "Kershaw's Brigade at Gettysburg," 45.

46. Hillyer, "Battle of Gettysburg," 9.

47. Ibid.

48. *OR*, vol. 27, pt. 2, 401–2.

49. Cochran, "Some Incidents on the March to Gettysburg," *Atlanta Journal*, August 31, 1901.

50. E. H. Sutton, *Civil War Stories* (Demorest, Ga.: Banner Printing Co., 1907), 42–45.

51. Parker, *Twenty-second Massachusetts*, 313; *OR*, vol. 27, pt. 1, 685.

52. Warner, *Generals in Blue*, 553; Tagg, *The Generals of Gettysburg*, 115–16; 118–19.

53. Tagg, *The Generals of Gettysburg*, 100–101.

54. *OR*, vol. 27, pt. 1, 653–54, 657, 684.

55. *OR*, vol. 27, pt. 1, 653; Pfanz, *Gettysburg: The Second Day*, 395.

56. Lafayette McLaws, "The Battle of Gettysburg," Paper Read before the Confederate Veterans Association, April 27, 1896, 80.

57. Bryan to McLaws, December 10, 1877, Southern Historical Collection.

58. Lafayette McLaws, "The Second Day at Gettysburg: General Sickles Answered by the Commander of the Opposing Forces the Federal Disaster of the Left," *Philadelphia Weekly Times*, August 4, 1886; James Longstreet, "Lee in Pennsylvania," *The Annals of the War* (Dayton, Ohio: Morningside House, Inc., 1988), 425.

59. *OR*, vol. 27, pt. 1, 684–85.

60. Pfanz, *Gettysburg: The Second Day*, 399–402; Hillyer, "Battle of Gettysburg," 9–10.

Chapter Seven

1. Robert Carter, *Four Brothers in Blue: A True Story of the Great Civil War from Bull Run to Appomattox* (Washington, D.C.: Gibson, 1913), 324–25.

2. See appendix A for Confederate troop casualties and appendix B for Federal troop casualties. All casualty figures taken from Busey and Martin, *Regimental Strengths and Losses*.

3. Anderson to Bachelder, *The Bachelder Papers*, 1:450.

4. Busey and Martin, *Regimental Strengths and Losses*, 135, 280, 298, 301.

5. W. E. James, in John K. McIver Chapter, United Daughters of the Confederacy, *Treasured Reminiscences* (Columbia, S.C.: The State Co. Printers, 1911), 27.

Bibliography

Manuscript Sources

Alabama State Archives

    J. C. Reid diary.

Domosh, Stan collection

    John Haley, *What I Saw at Gettysburg July 2 & 3, 1863*.

Duke University, William R. Perkins Library, Manuscript Department. Durham, N.C.

    Lafayette McLaws Papers.

Emory University Special Collections

    John A. Everett letter.

Fredericksburg and Spotsylvania National Military Park. Fredericksburg, Va.

    George W. Whipple, Memories of George W. Whipple Typescript.

Georgia Archives

    John Mounger letters.

Gettysburg National Military Park

    Kathleen R. Georg, May 1982 "Physical History and Analysis Section, Historic Structures, Report Rose Farmhouse."

    Kathy Georg Harrison, August 15, 1987, letter to Don Troiani.

The Historical Society of Pennsylvania. Philadelphia, Pa.

   Charles A. Hale, "With Colonel Cross in the Gettysburg Campaign," Miscellaneous Papers.

   John Rutter Brooke Papers.

   John L. Smith Papers.

      118th Pennsylvania Regiment, letter to Mother, July 9, 1863.

Indiana State Library

   Erasmus Gilbreath collection.

   "B. J. Worden's Gettysburg Experience" collection S1361.

Kennesaw Mountain National Military Park

   Diary of Marcus Green.

Kross, Gary collection

   Letter of Paul Semmes.

Library of Congress, Manuscript Division. Washington, D.C.

   Joshua L. Chamberlain Papers.

United States Army Military History Institute

   Daniel Gookin Journal, Lewis Leigh Collection.

University of Michigan, Michigan Historical Collection, Bentley Library

   Robert Campbell account.

   James Houghton Journal.

University of North Carolina, Southern Historical Society Collection. Chapel Hill, N.C.

   John Alexander Barry Papers.

   Franklin Gaillard Papers.

Zerbe, Steve collection

   Franklin I. Whitmore July 5, 1863, letter.

History of the Corn Exchange Regiment, 118th Pennsylvania Volunteers (Philadelphia: J. L. Smith, 1888).

Memorial to Samuel K. Zook. Philadelphia, Pa.: James Beale, printer, 1889, 16–17.

Newspapers

Atlanta Journal

Coos Democrat

Globe-Democrat

The News and Courier (Charleston)

Philadelphia Weekly Times

The Richmond Daily Enquirer

Richmond Sentinel

St. Louis Globe-Democrat

Tribune (Walton, Ga.)

Maps

Association of Licensed Battlefield Tour Guides, "The Second Day Seminar" maps.

Bachelder, John B. *Position of Troops, Second Day's Battle.* New York: Office of the Chief Engineers, U.S. Army, 1876.

Books, Articles, and Pamphlets

Abernathy, William M. *Our Mess: Southern Gallantry and Privations.* McKinney, Tex.: McKintex Press, 1977.

Acken, J. Gregory, ed. *Inside the Army of the Potomac: The Civil War Experience of Captain Francis Adams Donaldson.* Mechanicsburg, Pa.: Stackpole Books, 1998.

Adelman, Garry E., and Timothy H. Smith. *Devil's Den: A History and Guide.* Gettysburg, Pa.: Thomas Publications, 1997.

Aiken, David Wyatt. "The Gettysburg Reunion. What is Necessary and Proper for the South to Do. Open Letter from Col. D. Wyatt Aiken to Gen. J. B. Kershaw." *Charleston News and Courier,* June 21, 1882.

Alexander, Edward Porter. *Military Memoirs of a Confederate.* New York: Dayton, Ohio: Morningside Bookshop, 1977.

———. *Fighting for the Confederacy: The Personal Recollections of General Edward Porter Alexander*. Gary W. Gallagher, ed. Chapel Hill: University of North Carolina Press, 1989.

———. "The Great Charge and Artillery Fighting at Gettysburg." Robert U. Johnson and Clarence C. Buel, eds., *Battles and Leaders of the Civil War*. New York: Castle Books, 1956, vol. 3.

Annual Reports of the Gettysburg National Military Park Commission to the Secretary of War 1893–1904. Washington: Government Printing Office, 1905.

Aversano, Earl J. *Regimental History of the 8th New Jersey Volunteer Infantry*. Private publishing, n.d.

Bandy, Ken, and Florence Feeland, comps. *The Gettysburg Papers Volume II*. Dayton, Ohio: Morningside Bookshop, 1986.

Bertera, Martin, and Ken Oberholtzer. *The 4th Michigan Volunteer Infantry at Gettysburg: The Battle for the Wheatfield*. Dayton, Ohio: Morningside House, Inc., 1997.

Bigelow, John. *The Peach Orchard: Gettysburg, July 2, 1863*. Minneapolis: Kimball-Storer Co., 1919; reprint, Gaithersburg, Md.: Olde Soldier Books, Inc., 1987.

Boatner, Mark M., III. *The Civil War Dictionary*. New York: David McKay Company, Inc., 1987.

Brandt, Nat. *The Congressman Who Got Away with Murder*. New York: Syracuse University Press, 1991.

Busey, John W., and David G. Martin. *Regimental Strengths and Losses at Gettysburg*. Hightstown, N.J.: Longstreet House, 1986.

Campbell, Eric. "Baptism of Fire: The Ninth Massachusetts Battery at Gettysburg, July 2, 1863." *Gettysburg Magazine*, no. 5, July 1991.

———. "Caldwell Clears the Wheatfield." *Gettysburg Historical Articles of Lasting Interest*, no. 3, July 1990.

Campbell, Robert. "Pioneer Memories of the War Days 1861–1865." 30 *Michigan Pioneer and Historical Collections*, 1906.

Carter, Robert. *Four Brothers in Blue: A True Story of the Great Civil War from Bull Run to Appomattox.* Washington, D.C.: Gibson, 1913.

Catton, Bruce. *Gettysburg: The Final Fury.* Garden City, N.Y.: Doubleday & Company, Inc., 1974.

Cleaves, Freeman. *Meade of Gettysburg.* Dayton, Ohio: Morningside Bookshop, Inc., 1980.

Cochran, L. L. "Some Incidents on the March to Gettysburg." *Atlanta Journal*, August 31, 1901.

———. "The Tenth Georgia Regiment at Gettysburg." *Atlanta Journal*, February 23, 1901.

Coco, Gregory A. *On the Bloodstained Field: 130 Human Interest Stories of the Campaign and Battle of Gettysburg.* Gettysburg, Pa.: Thomas Publications, 1987.

———. *Killed in Action: Eyewitness Accounts of the Last Moments of 100 Union Soldiers Who Died at Gettysburg.* Gettysburg, Pa.: Thomas Publications, 1992.

Coddington, Edwin B. *The Gettysburg Campaign: A Study in Command.* New York: Charles Scribner's Sons, 1979.

Coffman, Richard. "A Vital Unit." *Civil War Times Illustrated*, 20 June, 1982.

Cole, Jacob H. *Under Five Commanders or A Boy's Experience with the Army of the Potomac.* Paterson, N.J.: News Printing Company, 1906.

Commonwealth of Pennsylvania. *Pennsylvania at Gettysburg Ceremonies at the Dedication of the Monuments*, 2 vols. Harrisburg, Pa.: W. M. Stanley Ray, 1904.

Conyngham, David Power. *The Irish Brigade and its Campaigns.* Lawrence Frederick Kohl, ed. New York: Fordham University Press, 1994.

Coxe, John. "The Battle of Gettysburg," *Confederate Veteran,* vol. 21, No. 9, 1913; reprint, Wilmington, N.C.: Broadfoot Publishing Company, 1990.

Crotty, Daniel G. *Four Years Campaigning in the Army of the Potomac.* Kearny, N.J.: Belle Grove Publishing Company, 1995.

Crute, Joseph H., Jr. *Units of the Confederate States Army.* Gaithersburg, Md.: Olde Soldier Books, Inc., 1987.

Current, Richard N. *Encyclopedia of the Confederacy,* 4 vols., New York: Simon & Schuster, Inc., 1993.

Dalton, Pete, and Cyndi Dalton. *Into the Valley of Death: The Story of the 4th Maine at Gettysburg.* Union, Maine: Union Publishing Company, 1994.

de Paris, Comte. *The Battle of Gettysburg.* Baltimore, Md.: Butternut and Blue, 1987.

de Trobriand, Regis. *Four Years with the Army of the Potomac.* Boston: Ticknor and Company, 1889; reprint, Gaithersburg, Md.: Ron R. Van Sickle Military Books, 1988.

Dickert, D. Augustus. *History of Kershaw's Brigade.* Newberry, S.C.: Elbert H. Hull Company, 1899; reprint, Dayton, Ohio: Morningside House, Inc., 1988.

Dowdey, Clifford. *Death of a Nation: The Story of Lee and His Men at Gettysburg.* Baltimore, Md.: Butternut and Blue, 1988.

Drake, S. A. *The Battle of Gettysburg.* Wilmington, N.C.: Broadfoot Publishing Company, 1988.

Evans, Clement A., ed. *Confederate Military History: Extended Edition,* 19 vols. Wilmington, N.C.: Broadfoot Publishing Company, 1987.

Everson, Guy R., and Edward H. Simpson, Jr., eds. *"Far, Far from Home": The Wartime Letters of Dick and Tally Simpson, 3rd South Carolina Volunteers.* New York: Oxford University Press, 1994.

Favill, Josiah Marshall. *The Diary of a Young Officer Serving with the Armies of the United States during the War of the Rebellion*. Chicago: R. R. Donnelly & Sons Company, 1909.

Figg, Royall W. *"Where Men Only Dare to Go!": Or the Story of a Boy Company by an Ex-Boy*. Richmond: Whittet and Shepperson, 1885.

Freeman, Douglas Southall. *R. E. Lee,* 4 vols. New York: Charles Scribner's Sons, 1934–35; reprint, New York: Charles Scribner's Sons, 1987.

————. *Lee's Lieutenants: A Study in Command,* 3 vols. New York: Charles Scribner's Sons, 1949–51; reprint, New York: Charles Scribner's Sons, 1970.

Fuller, Charles A. *Personal Recollections of the War of 1861*. Sherburne, N.Y.: New Job Printing House, 1906; reprint, Hamilton, N.Y.: Edmonston Publishing, Inc. 1990.

Gallagher, Gary W., ed. *The Second Day at Gettysburg: Essays on Confederate and Union Leadership*. Kent, Ohio: Kent State University Press, 1993.

Gambone, A. M. *Hancock at Gettysburg...and Beyond*. Baltimore, Md.: Butternut and Blue, 1997.

————. *The Life of General Samuel K. Zook: Another Forgotten Union Hero*. Baltimore, Md.: Butternut and Blue, 1996.

Griffin, John. *Warriors of the Wiregrass*. Moultrie, Ga.: private printing, 2000.

Hagerty, Edward J. *Collis' Zouaves: The 114th Pennsylvania Volunteers in the Civil War*. Baton Rouge and London: Louisiana State University Press, 1997.

Hamblen, Charles. *Connecticut Yankees at Gettysburg*. Walter L. Powell, ed. Kent, Ohio: Kent State University Press, 1993.

Hamilton, James C. M. "History of the 110th Pennsylvania Infantry Regiment." Military Order of the Loyal Legion of the U.S. Collection, Civil War Library and Museum, Philadelphia, Pa.

———. "The 110th Pennsylvania in the Gettysburg Campaign." *Philadelphia Weekly Press*, February 24, 1886.

Hanifer, Michael. *History of Battery B, First New Jersey Artillery*. Cottawa, Ill.: Republican Times Printers, 1905.

Hartwig, D. Scott. "'No Troops on the Field Had Done Better: John C. Caldwell's Division in the Wheatfield, July 2, 1863," in Gary Gallagher, ed., *The Second Day at Gettysburg: Essays on Confederate and Union Leadership*. Kent, Ohio: The Kent State University Press, 1993.

Hawthorne, Frederick W. *Gettysburg: Stories of Men and Monuments: As Told by Battlefield Guides*. Hanover, Pa.: Association of Licensed Battlefield Guides, 1988.

Hewett, Janet B., Noah Andre Trudeau, and Bryce A. Suderow, eds. *Supplement to the Official Records of the Union and Confederate Armies*. Wilmington, N.C.: Broadfoot Publishing, 1995.

Hillyer, George. "Battle of Gettysburg." Walton *Tribune*, August 2, 1904.

Hofe, Michael W. *That There Be No Stain upon My Stones*. Gettysburg, Pa.: Thomas Publications, 1995.

Hoke, Jacob. *The Great Invasion of 1863 or: General Lee in Pennsylvania*. Gettysburg, Pa.: Stan Clark Military Books, 1992.

Hood, John B. *Advance and Retreat: Personal Experiences in the United States and Confederate States Armies*. New Orleans: n.p., 1880.

Hudson, Travis. "Soldier Boys in Gray: A History of the 59th Georgia Volunteer Infantry Regiment." *Atlanta Journal*, vol. 23, no. 1, spring 1979.

Humphreys, Andrew. *Semmes America*. Memphis, Tenn.: Humphreys Ink, Inc., 1989.

Imhof, John D. *Gettysburg Day Two: A Study in Maps.* Baltimore, Md.: Butternut & Blue, 1999.

James, W. E., in John K. McIver Chapter, United Daughters of the Confederacy, *Treasured Reminiscences.* Columbia, S.C.: The State Co. Printers, 1911.

Johnson, Robert U., and Clarence C. Buel, eds. *Battles and Leaders of the Civil War,* 4 vols. New York: Century Company, 1884–89; reprint, New York: Castle Books, 1956.

Johnson, William. "Gettysburg." *Atlanta Journal.* Vertical Files, Fredericksburg and Spotsylvania National Military Park Library.

Jones, Charles Edgeworth. *Georgia in the War 1861–1865.* Fayetteville, Ga.: Americana Historical Books, 1994.

Jones, Paul. *The Irish Brigade.* Washington and New York: Robert B. Luce, Inc., 1969.

Jordan, William Barnes, Jr. "Gettysburg and the Seventeenth Maine." *Gettysburg Magazine,* no. 8, January 1993.

———. *Red Diamond Regiment: The 17th Maine Infantry, 1862–1865.* Shippensburg, Pa.: White Mane Publishing Company, Inc., 1996.

Jorgensen, Jay. "Anderson Attacks the Wheatfield." *Gettysburg Magazine,* no. 14, January 1996.

———. "Edward Porter Alexander, Confederate Cannoneer at Gettysburg." *Gettysburg Magazine,* no. 17, July 1997.

———. "Wofford Sweeps the Wheatfield." *Gettysburg Magazine,* no. 22, January 2000.

Joslyn, Mauriel Phillips. *Charlotte's Boys: Civil War Letters of the Branch Family of Savannah.* Berryville, Va.: Rockbridge Publishing Company, 1996.

Kershaw, Joseph. "Kershaw's Brigade at Gettysburg." In *Battles and Leaders of the Civil War.* Robert U. Johnson and Clarence C. Buel, eds. New York: Castle Books, 1956.

Krick, Robert K. *Lee's Colonels: A Biographical Register of the Field Officers of the Army of Northern Virginia.* 4th ed., Dayton, Ohio: Morningside House, Inc., 1992.

Kross, Gary. "Rebel Yells on Both Flanks." *Blue & Gray Magazine*, vol. 5, March 1988.

———. "To Die Like Soldiers: The Retreat from Sickles' Front, July 2, 1863." *Blue & Gray Magazine*, vol. 15, July 1998.

Ladd, David L., and Audrey J. Ladd. *John Bachelder's History of the Battle of Gettysburg.* Dayton, Ohio: Morningside House, Inc., 1997.

———. *The Bachelder Papers: Gettysburg in Their Own Words*, 3 vols. Dayton, Ohio: Morningside House, Inc., 1994.

Large, George R. *Battle of Gettysburg: The Official History by the Gettysburg National Military Park Commission.* Shippensburg, Pa.: Burd Street Press, 1999.

Law, Evander M. "The Struggle for Round Top." In *Battles and Leaders of the Civil War*. Robert U. Johnson and Clarence C. Buel, eds. New York: Castle Books, 1956.

Longstreet, James. *From Manassas to Appomattox.* Philadelphia: J. B. Lippincott, 1896; reprint, New York: DeCupo Press, 1992.

———. "Lee in Pennsylvania." In *The Annals of the War*. Philadelphia: Times Publishing Company, 1879; reprint, Dayton, Ohio: Morningside House, Inc., 1988.

Luvaas, Jay. *The U.S. Army War College Guide to the Battle of Gettysburg.* Carlisle, Pa.: South Mountain Press, Inc., 1987.

Marcot, Ray. "Berdan Sharpshooters at Gettysburg." *Historical Articles of Lasting Interest*, no. 1, July 1989.

Martin, James M. *History of the Fifty-Seventh Pennsylvania Veteran Volunteers.* Kearny, N.J.: Belle Grove Publishing, Company, 1995.

McDonald, JoAnna M. *The World Will Long Remember: A Guide to the Battle of Gettysburg.* Shippensburg, Pa.: White Mane Publishing Company, Inc., 1996.

―――. *The Faces of Gettysburg: Photographs from the Gettysburg National Military Park Library.* Redondo Beach, Calif.: Rank and File Publications, 1997.

McLaws, Lafayette. "Gettysburg." *Southern Historical Society Papers.* Dayton, Ohio: Broadfoot Publishing Company/ Morningside House, 1990.

―――. "The Battle of Gettysburg." Paper Read Before the Confederate Veterans Association, April 27, 1896.

McLean, James L., and Judy W. McLean. *Gettysburg Sources.* Vol. 2, Baltimore, Md.: Butternut and Blue, 1988.

McNeily, J. S. *Barksdale's Mississippi Brigade at Gettysburg: "Most Magnificent Charge of the War.* Gaithersburg, Md.: Olde Soldier Books, Inc., 1987.

Meade, George. *The Life and Letters of George Gordon Meade,* 2 vols. New York: Charles Scribner's Sons, 1913.

Michigan at Gettysburg: Proceedings Incident to the Dedication of the Michigan Monuments upon the Battlefield of Gettysburg, June 12, 1889. Detroit. Mich.: Winn & Hammon, 1889.

Miller, Robert C. *Historic Views of Gettysburg.* Gettysburg, Pa.: J. I. Mumper & R. C. Miller, 1915.

Montgomery, James Stuart. *The Shaping of a Battle: Gettysburg.* Philadelphia and New York: Chilton Company, 1959.

Muffly, J. W. *The Story of Our Regiment: A History of the 148th Pennsylvania Volunteers.* Des Moines: Kenyon Printing & Manufacturing Company, 1904; reprint, Baltimore, Md.: Butternut and Blue, 1994.

Mulholland, St. Clair A. *The Story of the 116th Regiment Pennsylvania Volunteers.* Lawrence Frederick Kohl, ed. New York: Fordham University Press, 1996.

Murphy, T. L. *Kelly's Heroes: The Irish Brigade at Gettysburg.* Gettysburg, Pa.: Farnsworth House Military Impressions, 1997.

New York Monuments Commission for the Battlefields of Gettysburg and Chattanooga. *Final Report on the Battlefield of Gettysburg.* 3 vols. Albany: J. B. Lyon Company, 1900.

Nicholson, John P., ed. *Pennsylvania at Gettysburg: Ceremonies at the Dedication of the Monuments Erected by the Commonwealth of Pennsylvania to Mark the Positions of the Pennsylvania Commands Engaged in the Battle.* 2 vols. Harrisburg, Pa.: W. S. Ray, State Printer, 1904.

O'Brien, Kevin E. "Into the Wheatfield: The Union Army's Irish Brigade at Gettysburg." Vertical Files, Gettysburg National Military Park Library.

Parker, Francis J. *The Story of the Thirty-Second Regiment Massachusetts Infantry.* Boston: C. W. Calkins & Co., 1880.

Parker, John L. *Henry Wilson's Regiment: History of the Twenty-Second Massachusetts Infantry, the Second Company Sharpshooters and the Third Light Battery, in the War of the Rebellion.* Boston: Press of Rand Avery Company, 1887; reprint, Baltimore, Md.: Butternut and Blue, 1996.

Pfanz, Harry W. *Gettysburg: The Second Day.* Chapel Hill: University of North Carolina Press, 1987.

Polley, J. B. *Hood's Texas Brigade: Its Marches, Its Battles, Its Achievements.* New York: Neale Publishing Company, 1910; reprint, Dayton, Ohio: Morningside House, Inc., 1988.

Powell, William H. *The Fifth Army Corps.* New York: G. P. Putnam's Sons, 1896; reprint, Dayton, Ohio: Morningside House, Inc., 1984.

Rauch, William. *History of the Bucktails.* Dayton, Ohio: Morningside House, Inc., 1988.

Reese, Timothy J. *Sykes' Regular Infantry Division, 1861–1864.* Jefferson, N.C., and London: McFarland & Company, Inc., 1990.

Ridinger, William. "The Wheatfield, A Harvest of Death." 1990. Personal Collection, A. M. Gambone.

Robertson, John, ed. *Michigan in the War*. Lansing, Mich.: George, 1882.

Robins, Richard. "The Regular Troops at Gettysburg." *Philadelphia Weekly Times*, January 4, 1879.

Rogers, Thomas Blackburn. "St. Louisians among Gettysburg Heros." *Globe-Democrat*, March 9, 1913.

Rollins, Richard. *Guide to Pennsylvania Troops at Gettysburg*. Redondo Beach, Calif.: Rank and File Publications, 1996.

———. *"The Damned Red Flags of the Rebellion": The Confederate Battle Flag at Gettysburg*. Redondo Beach, Calif.: Rank and File Publications, 1996.

Sauers, Richard A. *A Caspian Sea of Ink: The Meade-Sickles Controversy*. Baltimore, Md.: Butternut and Blue, 1989.

Sauers, Richard, ed. *Fighting Them Over How the Veterans Remembered Gettysburg in the Pages of The National Tribune*. Baltimore, Md.: Butternut and Blue, 1998.

Sheldon, Winthrop D. *The "Twenty-Seventh": A Regimental History*. New Haven: Morris & Benham, 1866.

Sherry, Jeffrey F. "The Terrible Impetuosity: The Pennsylvania Reserves at Gettysburg." *Gettysburg Magazine*, no. 16, January 1997.

Shumate, William T. "With Kershaw at Gettysburg." *Philadelphia Times Weekly*, May 6, 1882.

Sifakis, Stewart. *Who Was Who in the Civil War*. New York and Oxford: Facts on File Publications, 1988.

Smith, Gerald J. *"One of the Most Daring of Men": The Life of Confederate General William Tatum Wofford*. Murfreesboro, Tenn.: Southern Heritage Press, 1997.

Steiner, Paul E. *Physician-Generals in the Civil War*. Springfield, Ill.: Charles C. Thomas Publisher, 1966.

Stevens, Charles A. *Berdan's United States Sharpshooters in the Army of the Potomac.* St. Paul: The Price McGill Company, 1892; reprint, Dayton, Ohio: Morningside House, Inc., 1984.

Stewart, Robert L. *History of the One Hundred and Fortieth Regiment.* ———, Pa.: Regimental Association, 1912.

Storrick, W. C. *Gettysburg: Battle & Battlefield.* Harrisburg, Pa.: McFarland Company, 1969; reprint, New York: Barnes & Noble Books, 1993.

Styple, William B., ed. *Our Noble Blood: The Civil War Letters of Major-General Regis de Trobriand.* Kearny, N.J.: Belle Grove Publishing Co., 1997.

Sutton, E. H., *Civil War Stories.* Demorest, Ga.: Banner Printing Co., 1907.

Swanberg, W. A. *Sickles the Incredible.* New York: Charles Scribner's Sons, 1956; reprint, Gettysburg, Pa.: Stan Clark Military Books, 1991.

Symonds, Craig L. *Gettysburg: A Battlefield Atlas.* Baltimore, Md.: The Nautical & Aviation Publishing Company of America, 1992.

Tagg, Larry. *The Generals of Gettysburg.* Mason City, Iowa: Savas Publishing Company, 1998.

Thaxton, Candler H. *My Dear Wife from Your Devoted Husband: Letters from a Rebel Soldier to his Wife.* Warrington, Fla.: privately printed.

Toombs, Samuel. *New Jersey Troops in the Gettysburg Campaign.* Orange, N.J.: Evening Mail Publishing House, 1888; reprint, Hightstown, N.J.: Longstreet House, 1988.

Tremain, Henry Edwin. *Two Days of War: A Gettysburg Narrative and Other Excursions.* New York: Bonnell, Silvers and Bowers, 1905.

Tucker, Glenn. *Hancock the Superb.* Indianapolis: Bobbs-Merrill Company, 1960; reprint, Dayton, Ohio: Morningside House, Inc., 1980.

United States War Department. *The War of the Rebellion: A Compilation of the Official Records of the Union and Confederate Armies.* 70 vols. in 128 pts., Washington, D.C.: Government Printing Office, 1880–1901.

Vanderslice, J. M. *Gettysburg Then & Now.* New York: G. W. Dillingham Company, 1899.

Verrill, George W. "The Seventeenth Maine at Gettysburg and in the Wilderness." In Ken Bandy and Florence Freeland, comps., *The Gettysburg Papers.* Dayton, Ohio: Morningside, 1986.

Walker, Francis A. *History of the Second Army Corps.* New York: Charles Scribner's Sons, 1886; reprint, Gaithersburg, Md.: Olde Soldier Books, Inc., 1997.

Walters, Sara Gould. *Inscription at Gettysburg: In Memoriam to Capt. David Acheson, Company C, 140th Pennsylvania.* Gettysburg, Pa.: Thomas Publications, 1991.

Warner, Ezra J. *Generals in Blue: Lives of the Union Commanders.* Baton Rouge: Louisana State University Press, 1964; reprint, Baton Rouge: Louisiana State University Press, 1991.

———. *Generals in Gray: Lives of the Confederate Commanders.* Baton Rouge: Louisiana State University Press, 1959; reprint, Baton Rouge: Louisiana State University Press, 1988.

Welsch, Jack D. *Medical Histories of Confederate Generals.* Kent, Ohio: The Kent State University Press, 1995.

Wert, Jeffry D. *General James Longstreet: The Confederacy's Most Controversial Soldier.* New York: Simon & Schuster, 1993.

Wert, J. Howard. *Guide to the Positions on the Gettysburg Battlefield.* Harrisburg, Pa.: R. M. Sturgeon & Company, 1886.

West, John C. *A Texan in Search of a Fight: 4th Texas Infantry.* Waco: Press of J. S. Hill & Company, 1901; reprint, Baltimore, Md.: Butternut and Blue, 1994.

Wheeler, Richard. *Witness to Gettysburg.* New York: Harper & Row Publishers, 1987.

Wise, Jennings Cropper. *The Long Arm of Lee.* 2 vols. Richmond, Va.: Owens Publishing Company, 1988.

Wyckoff, Mac. *A History of the 2nd South Carolina Infantry: 1861–1865.* Fredericksburg, Va.: Sergeant Kirkland: Museum and Historical Society, Inc., 1994.

———. *A History of the 3rd South Carolina Infantry: 1861-1865.* Fredericksburg, Va.: Sergeant Kirkland: Museum and Historical Society, Inc., 1995.

———. "Kershaw's Brigade at Gettysburg." *The Gettysburg Magazine,* no. 5, July 1991.

Index

First names are listed where known.

A

Abbott, Ira C., 79
Aiken, David Wyatt, 7, 73, 98, 99
Alexander, Edward Porter, 28, 29, 71
Ames, Adelbert, 101
Ames, Nelson, 37
Anderson's Brigade, 33, 38, 50, 52, 53,
    55, 61, 92, 99, 103, 105, 117, 124,
    125, 130, 133
Anderson, George T., 131, 134
  battle, 59, 81, 83
  biographical, 2, 3, 134
  initial attack, 63, 67, 69, 70, 71, 75, 79,
    80, 86, 104, 107, 116, 131
  pre-battle preparations, 34, 49
Ashby's Gap, Virginia, 17, 18
Ayres, Romeyn B., 114, 117, 122

B

Bachelder, John, 33, 58
Bacon, Thomas Glascock, 7
Bailey, William P., 107
Ball, Edward, 12
Baltimore Pike, Pennsylvania, 95
Barclay, Elihu Stuart, Jr., 15
Barclay, William P., 16
Barksdale, William, 32, 33, 71, 108, 133
Barnes, James, 64, 65, 66, 67, 79, 81, 82,
    96, 97, 114, 115
Barri, Thomas, 122
Barry, John Alexander, 108, 112
Barto, Ben H., 57
Bass, Muston G., 53
Beauregard, Pierre Gustave Toutant, 6
Bell, Charles A., 51
Benning, Henry L., 33, 49, 94, 104, 119,
    124, 130, 131, 135
Bentley, Richard C., 99
Berdan, Hiram, 36

Biesecker's Woods, Pennsylvania 33, 36,
    75
Bigelow, John, 37, 74, 78, 79, 81
Big Round Top, Pennsylvania, 37
Birney, David B., 38, 63, 70, 84, 96
Black Horse Tavern, Pennsylvania, 27,
    28, 29, 71
Bland, Elbert, 98
Brewer, Samuel, 26
Brewster, William R., 37
Briscoe, Joseph C., 84
Brooke, John R., 88, 90, 101, 104, 105,
    107, 116, 117
Broom, Charles H. H., 95
Brown, Hiram Louis, 103
Brown, Jack, 4, 52
Brown, Joseph, 9, 10, 13
Bryan, Goode, 14, 109, 130
Buchanan, James, 14
Buckley, John, 110
Bucklyn, John K., 36
Buford, John, 24
Burbank, Sydney, 114, 117, 119, 122
Burling, George C., 57, 58, 59, 60, 61, 67
Butler, Benjamin, 22

C

Caldwell, John C., 2, 86, 87, 88, 90, 91,
    101, 107, 112, 114, 119
Caledonia Iron Works, Pennsylvania, 24
Campbell, Eric, 2
Campbell, Robert, 154 n. 25
Cash, Ellerbe Boggan Crawford, 7
Cashtown Gap, Pennsylvania, 25
Cemetery Hill, Pennsylvania, 26
Cemetery Ridge, Pennsylvania, 26, 35,
    36, 63, 79, 88, 125, 127, 131
Chambersburg, Pennsylvania, 17, 23, 24
Chambersburg Pike, 24

172

The Author

JAY JORGENSEN earned a bachelor's degree in history from Fairleigh Dickinson University and received his juris doctorate from Villanova University School of Law. He has a master of arts degree in military history and Civil War studies from American Military University. He is a partner in the law firm of Jorgensen & Barnes and also serves as a municipal court judge in New Jersey. Jay is a frequent presenter at Civil War Round Tables and has had numerous articles published in *Gettysburg Magazine*. He lives in Colonia, New Jersey, with his wife and two sons.